PREACHING THROUGH THE CHRISTIAN YEAR
10

PREACHING THROUGH THE CHRISTIAN YEAR 10

Sermons from Queens' College, Cambridge

Brian Hebblethwaite

*Fellow, Dean of Chapel, and Director of Studies in
Philosophy, Theology and Religious Studies,
Queens' College, Cambridge*

MOWBRAY
LONDON & OXFORD

ISBN 0 264 67061 2

First published 1985
by A.R. Mowbray & Co. Ltd,
Saint Thomas House, Becket Street,
Oxford, OX1 1SJ

Typeset by Comersgate Art Studios, Oxford
Printed in Great Britain by Biddles Ltd, Guildford

British Library Cataloguing in Publication Data

Preaching through the Christian year.—(Mowbray's
    sermon outline series)
    10 : Sermons from Queens' College, Cambridge
    1. Church of England—Sermons   2. Church year
    sermons—Outlines, syllabi, etc.
    I. Hebblethwaite, Brian   II. Queens' College,
    Cambridge
    251'.01   BX5133

ISBN 0-264-67061-2

CONTENTS

v

ACKNOWLEDGEMENTS

Extracts from the Book of Common Prayer 1662, which is Crown Copyright in the United Kingdom, are reproduced by permission of Eyre & Spottiswoode (Publishers) Limited, Her Majesty's Printers London.

Extracts from *Contemporary Transformations of Religion* by Bryan Wilson (1979) are reproduced by permission of Oxford University Press.

Extracts from one of the *Vatican II Conciliar and Postconciliar Documents* are reproduced by permission of Dominican Publications.

Extracts from *Brideshead Revisited* by Evelyn Waugh are reproduced by permission of A. D. Peters & Co. Ltd on behalf of the Estate of Evelyn Waugh.

An extract from *The End of Man* by Austin Farrer is reproduced by permission of the Society for Promoting Christian Knowledge.

Biblical quotations are from the Revised Standard Version.

PREFACE

Most of these sermons were preached in the Chapel of Queens' College, Cambridge. In my experience, students do not like too academic a sermon, but they do appreciate clear exposition of Christian belief and of what being a Christian involves in the world today. Inevitably, my being a philosopher of religion by trade has given these sermons something of a bias towards the theoretical side of Christian faith, but I hope that the connection between theory and practice comes through clearly enough.

My college has recently been exposed to public scrutiny through the medium of television, and it occurred to me that this might be an opportunity to share my conviction of the intelligibility and importance of Christian belief and of Christian ethics with a wider audience. At the very least it may be of some interest to see how these central questions strike a philosophical theologian who still believes in an objective God, the creator of heaven and earth.

B.H.

1

CREATION

I want to say something about the Christian doctrine of creation. Please do not be put off by this word 'doctrine'. Although we talk in words, we are not thinking about words. 'The doctrine of creation' is just shorthand for the way Christians think and ponder and achieve insight into, not words, but creation itself. What we are to think about is the world God has made – the world, including ourselves, in dependence on its creator and sustainer – in dependence, that is, for its being in being, for its order and evolution, and for its ultimate future.

There are many ways of looking at the world, and the religions of the world have fostered several of them. The physical world has been thought of as a prison of the soul, as basically illusory, as the playful outpouring of divine energy, as a school for the fashioning of persons. Christianity has from time to time embraced elements from all these views, but its fundamental teaching has always been that the world and ourselves as part of the world are creatures – real, but dependent beings – created out of nothing, existing with a derived being, depending for our being in being and our remaining in being on the creative loving will of God, the infinite uncreated source and sustainer of the world and ourselves.

I should like to say a word about three aspects of creation, first about this basic fact of our dependence, then about God's continuing creative work throughout the whole world process, and thirdly about the future goal of creation.

1 *The world's dependence on God for its existence*
Well, firstly, our sheer dependence on God for our being here

1

at all. This is the first thing to think about. Genesis one and two, in their different ways, tell us stories to bring out this fundamental religious insight into the dependence of all creatures, including ourselves, on God's creative will. They are stories, not literal factual accounts, but stories of great profundity and insight, bringing home to the religious imagination the dependence of the world for its very being on God. This is a source of wonder and gratitude for us. Mystics down the ages have expressed this wonder. Contemplating a stone or a leaf, let alone a human being, they have realized vividly, in their meditations, the wonder of the being of this creature – this leaf or whatever it may be. Just listen to the seventeenth century mystic Thomas Traherne.

'You never enjoy the world aright, till every morning you awake in heaven, see yourself in your Father's Palace; and look upon the skies, the earth and the air as Celestial Joys: having such a reverend esteem of all, as if you were among the Angels. . . . You never enjoy the world aright, till the Sea itself floweth in your veins, till you are clothed with the heavens, and crowned with the stars: and perceive yourself to be the sole heir of the whole world, and more so, because men are in it who are every one, sole heirs as well as you. Till you sing and rejoice and delight in God, as misers do in gold, and Kings in sceptres, you never enjoy the world. Till your spirit filleth the whole world, and the stars are your jewels; till you are as familiar with the ways of God in all Ages as with your walk and table: till you are intimately acquainted with the shady nothing out of which the world was made: till you love men so as to desire their happiness, with a thirst equal to the zeal of your own; till you delight in God for being good to all: you never enjoy the world. Till you remember how lately you were made, and how wonderful it was when you came into it: and more rejoice in the palace of your glory than if it had been made but today morning.'

Well, there is a man who could celebrate creation. At the very least, it is worth contemplating the potentialities of human consciousness for coming out with that sort of thing. When you think of our everyday forms of consciousness, you may well conclude that we are not exercising our God-given powers very much these days.

That rhapsodic passage has taken us somewhat beyond my first point which was simply to dwell on the dependence of every created thing on God for its very being.

2 God's continuing work in creation

But next we need to contemplate the order and evolution of the cosmos. For this too ultimately stems, according to the Judaeo-Christian vision, from the ongoing creative work of God. The world is not just set in being and left to its own devices. It is rather a process of continuous creation – a process of ever new development, its structures giving birth to ever new forms of created being: matter, life, consciousness, personality, spirit. We need a vision of creation such as that of the French Jesuit, Teilhard de Chardin, with its comprehensive sweep, and sense of the whole movement of creation from the initial burst of energy (or its constant renewal – though this seems less plausible now), through the formation of the galaxies and suns and planetary systems, through the appearance of living matter and its manifold evolution, until creatures appeared capable of looking out into infinity and responding freely and personally to their maker. Shaping this whole process, the religious consciousness perceives the hidden hand of God. Moreover the structure that sustains our life on earth – the laws of nature, the regular seasons, the fruits of the earth – all these can be seen to manifest the creator's ongoing activity. The men of Israel did not take all this for granted: they recognized the threat of chaos behind the order of the world, and in the story of the flood they painted a picture of the breakdown of that order. Life and the conditions that make life possible are God's to take away. Thus, once again, our dependence on God is vividly portrayed. You remember at the end of that

3

story God makes a covenant with Noah, and sets the rainbow in the sky as a sign of his promise to mankind. 'While the earth remains, seedtime and harvest, cold and heat, summer and winter, day and night, shall not cease.' So for our continuing in being, as for our very existence, we depend on God's faithfulness.

3 *The future of creation*

But the third aspect of creation is the future. Just as we depend on God for our existence, and for our continuing in being in the context of an evolving world, so it is he who sets the goal of the whole process. Now we can exult in creation after the manner of Treherne, we can trace the hidden hand of God's providence in the whole world process in which we find ourselves, but it is manifest that the creation is incomplete. Out of this stupendous process something is being fashioned. Paul in Romans 8 speaks of the creation groaning like a woman in travail. The creation as we know it is in process of giving birth, and our religious response is quite insufficient if we have no eye for God's future. The Bible is full of imagery of the future – of the day of the Lord, when the lion will lie down with the lamb, and the heavenly Jerusalem will descend with the river of the water of life, sparkling like crystal, flowing from the throne of God. And the voice proclaims: 'Behold, the dwelling of God is with men. He will dwell with them, and they shall be his people, and God himself will be with them; he will wipe away every tear from their eyes, and death shall be no more, neither shall there be mourning nor crying nor pain any more; for the former things have passed away.'

If I had time, I should want to say much more about the problem of evil here. That is the problem for any doctrine of creation; and it has to be faced up to, if our faith is not to have a hollow ring. We cannot just live in the world of Traherne. But the problem of evil is too large a topic to launch into here. All I will say is that somehow we have to realize that, as well

4

as being fundamentally good in itself, a physical, material world such as this is the necessary condition for the achievement of God's purpose. In other words, God's future kingdom could not be created direct, but requires the kind of build-up which we experience now, despite its by-products of evil and suffering. That is a difficult view to sustain, but not impossible, I think.

To return to the subject in hand – you may think that there is very little to be said about God's future; the ultimate future of God's creation is concealed from us here and now. But that would be to reckon without Easter. So far I have not really mentioned anything specifically Christian in what I have said about creation, and indeed we share the doctrine of creation with our Jewish and our Muslim friends. But, for Christians, faith in God's future is possible now, just because of the resurrection of our Lord Jesus Christ from the dead. That is why every Eucharist, as well as being a memorial of Christ's death, is also a celebration of God's future. This is the specifically Christian turn given to the doctrine of creation – its future hope and assurance, based on our Easter faith. And a lot more springs from this than I have got time to talk about today. Remember what Paul says in Colossians 1, where he spells out the further Christian insight that the one who was crucified and rose again was the one through whom the worlds were made, in whom all things are held together, and the one who is to be in all things alone supreme. In the imagery of Revelation, in the heavenly Jerusalem, on the throne, is the Lamb.

So, you see, all three aspects of creation, past, present and future, can be given a much more specifically Christian shape than I gave them in my initial exposition.

4 *Creation and science*
One final footnote: nothing that I have said to you today about creation need conflict with science. The idea that there is necessarily conflict between science and religion over

5

creation is based on ignorance. If we want to learn about cosmology, the structure of matter or physical causation, well, there are plenty of people here in Cambridge working in radio astronomy and elementary particle physics who can tell us about that. But I dare say they would be the first to admit that they can tell us nothing about the ultimate source of the being and nature of things or about their meaning and purpose. Nor can they tell us about the ultimate future of things; for their prognostications are inevitably based on present structures, whereas Christian talk of the future is based on the recreative power of God.

Consequently we must feel free to celebrate the gift of being – our being here, the being of the stars and sun, earth, fire, air and water, sand and stone, and grass and leaves, leaping salmon, whales and kittens, and the creative work of man in paint and music and words, in stone and glass and steel, creative work in which man faintly images the divine creator. We must feel free to celebrate the order of the seasons, the resources of energy which man will, I hope, discover and learn to use sensibly, the sources of innovation and experiment in problem solving and fashioning a humane and just society. We must feel free to celebrate the resurrection and the ultimate future – the heavenly city into which God in his good time will transform his creation.

2

JESUS

I suppose you could define a Christian as a follower of Jesus Christ. There are innumerable ways of being a follower of Jesus Christ and many degrees of commitment to him.

Christians think of him in many different ways too. I hope that the Christian Church is large and broad enough to embrace and welcome anyone who, in any way and to any degree, is attracted or inspired by the figure of Jesus Christ, anyone who in any way wishes to be counted a member of the Christian body. But, of course, we hope, too, that all who feel something of that attraction, something of that inspiration, will grow into a fuller and fuller knowledge of Jesus Christ, who he is, and what he means for us and for the world.

1 *The teaching and example of Jesus*
What is it about Jesus that attracts and inspires even after nearly two thousand years? Certainly his teaching and his example, as we read about them in the Gospels. I think many people still feel that there has never been any teaching like his – those astonishing parables about the kingdom of God, those piercing sayings about purity of heart, forgiveness, and gratitude to God, that confident teaching that God is close to us like a father, that God is in our midst, within us even, that God both gives himself to us and expects everything from us, that God comforts us and enables us to love without reserve. It is indeed astonishing, powerful teaching, and there has never been anything like it before or since.

The example of Jesus too retains its compelling power to attract and inspire – his single-minded devotion to God and his neighbour, his fearless confrontation of hypocrisy and hate, and yet his willingness to go the way of the cross rather than fight back, his words on the cross: Father, forgive them; for they know not what they do. This example of love, truth and endurance haunts our imaginations as we read and meditate upon the story of Christ's passion.

For some people it is simply that wonderful teaching and that compelling example that make them want to associate themselves with the Church and call themselves Christians. And of course we welcome them and call them our Christian brothers and sisters.

7

2 *The divinity of Jesus Christ*

But neither they nor we can turn a blind eye to the fact that Christians down the ages have wanted to say more than this about Jesus Christ. In our creeds and our hymns and our prayers we speak of him as our saviour and our God. Now, what is it that makes us think of Jesus Christ as more than just a wonderful teacher and a compelling pattern for our lives?

It is not something we can just read in the story of Jesus from the beginning of his ministry in Galilee to his death on the Cross outside Jerusalem, as we find it told in the Gospels – at least not if we study the Gospels carefully and critically. Admittedly there are features in that story which, even on critical study, differentiate him from the prophets and the saints through whom God spoke before and since. The authority with which he taught, his lack of any sense at all of any unworthiness, his calm assumption of the right to forgive, his power to make men whole – these are striking features of his life and ministry on earth. But we have to remember that the gospel tale is told by men who had already come to think of him as their saviour and their God, men who looked back on his life from their subsequent experience of his resurrection and his presence with them in spirit and in sacrament. These were the things that had opened their eyes to who he really was.

As we consider the question who Jesus really was, I think we have to give a great deal of weight to this astonishing fact that within a few years of his ignominious death, his disillusioned and scattered disciples were turning the world upside down with their preaching of Christ crucified and risen, and speaking of him as their saviour and their God. Nothing less than the resurrection and the experience of Christ as alive and active by his Spirit in their midst can have effected this amazing transformation.

3 *Experience of the living Christ*

But again I do not think that the power of Jesus to attract followers today as in all ages since his time can be explained simply by speaking of the witnesses of his resurrection and the experience of the first Christians. Certainly they had cause to recognize in him more than a great teacher and example; for they experienced him as risen and alive. But Christian faith today is still experience of Jesus Christ as risen and alive. This is the crucial point for us. We share in the body of Christian believers who, ever since those days nearly two thousand years ago, have known Jesus Christ as a living saviour and lord. No more than the early Christians do we think of Jesus as just a figure from the past. It is this continuing living relation, by prayer and sacrament, between the followers of Jesus and the one whose followers they are, that sustains our Christian faith that in Jesus we have to do not only with an inspiring teacher and a compelling example, but our saviour and our God. This is the point. We share through prayer and sacrament something of that *present* experience of Christ which transformed the first followers of Jesus from disillusionment into the apostles of a new age.

Now as we reflect on Jesus Christ from the point of view of people who participate through prayer and sacrament in his risen life, we begin to see what is meant by speaking of Jesus both as saviour and as God. For those who experience communion with the living Lord it is quite impossible to distinguish or separate Jesus from God. We are reconciled into a living relationship to God by God himself coming amongst us as one of us. We realize that Jesus is indeed Emmanuel – God with us – God manifesting himself to us in human form, in an approachable form. God saves us from our sins precisely by refusing to remain aloof, but rather by coming into our very midst, taking the burden of evil and suffering on himself, showing us the cost of the divine forgiveness and love, and pouring the Spirit of Christ crucified and risen into our hearts, as we respond in gratitude

9

and love. All this is God's own doing. It is God himself whom we hear in the teaching of Jesus; it is God himself who suffers on the cross; it is God himself who comes to us in the Spirit and in the body and blood of Christ.

4 *The doctrine of the incarnation*

I think it makes all the difference in the world – and this is what is special about Christianity – if we can see Christ's cross as God's cross in our world. I think that God is credible, knowable, reliable and lovable, precisely because, without in any way ceasing to be the God he ever is, he takes our nature upon him, comes amongst us as one of us, and loves us even at the cost of the passion and the cross.

I also think that this Christian doctrine of the incarnation is the only thing that really makes sense of the uniqueness of Jesus' teaching, his sinlessness, his perfect knowledge of God the Father, his resurrection, his living presence in the Spirit and the sacrament, as he is present whenever we pray, whenever we meet together for worship, and whenever we receive the sacrament.

Of course there are difficulties for our understanding in this doctrine of the incarnation. I have spoken of Jesus Christ as God made man, and yet also of the man Jesus' perfect knowledge of God the Father. And indeed we have to think of Jesus' prayers to the Father as manifesting to us in human terms the inner relations of love given and love received within the blessed Trinity. Our understanding of God cannot remain the same once God reveals himself in and as a man who prays to God. But these implications of Christian belief in Jesus Christ as God incarnate – this understanding of God in trinitarian terms – is too big a subject to go into now. It is enough for today if we can see something of how the attraction of the figure of Jesus the Galilean teacher and the man of sorrows on the cross depends on his being the human face of God, the living revelation and presence of God himself to us, both then and now.

3

AN INCARNATIONAL RELIGION

When I went to a college production of *The Merchant of Venice* the other week, no sooner had I taken my seat and opened my programme, than I found myself reading a somewhat pointed quotation from the play, which they printed at the foot of the page on which the cast was listed:

'It is a good divine that follows his own instruction.'

Now I can hardly take this as a text for my address to you this evening, for two reasons: one, that I do not think that I am very good at following my own instruction, and the other, that I do not like sermons in which the preacher talks about himself. I have always regarded it as the preacher's task to point away from himself to the wonder of God and of God's acts in creating the world, in redeeming mankind, and in inspiring man to live creatively and lovingly in the world.

So I'll take the liberty of tampering with Shakespeare and rewriting the line, so that it will serve more readily the theme I want to dwell on here tonight:

'It is good divinity to see what follows from the doctrine.'

The scansion is not so good, but never mind.

1 *Belief in the incarnation*
I find myself thinking and writing these days a great deal about the doctrine of the incarnation. I deeply distrust the common view in modern theology and the plain man's mind that Jesus was just a good man, especially close to God, whose example, both ethically and spiritually, we should

11

follow. To think like that, to my mind, is to miss the central insight in the Christian vision – namely, that in Jesus Christ we have to do with God himself, with God in one of the modes of his being, coming amongst us, without ceasing to be God, and making himself known in revelation and grace, by personal presence here in our midst, this side of the gap between finite and infinite, time and eternity. For it is the incarnation which enables us to comprehend the mysterious and strictly incomprehensible God, who is the source and goal of all created being, and at the same time enables us to realize that God takes on himself the ultimate responsibility for all the world's evil, by suffering its agony himself on our behalf. (To return to Shakespeare – one might say that Jesus Christ is 'a good divine that follows his own instruction' – though that, of course, would be to use the word 'divine' more literally than in its sense of a teacher of divinity.)

Well, it is this doctrine of the incarnation of which I now want to ask, what follows from it? What follows from the doctrine of the incarnation?

2 *A sacramental view of the world*
There are many profound consequences. In the first place the belief that 'the Word became flesh and dwelt among us' has profound consequences for our whole attitude to the world and to man. Granted that the purpose of the incarnation was to make possible something new, something which the New Testament writers speak of as reconciliation, recreation, salvation, nevertheless it was into this material, physical world that the Son of God came. An incarnational religion cannot despise the material, physical world any more than it can the humanity in which God made himself present for our sakes. Our humanity after all is bodily existence; we are deeply rooted in the natural physical world. And the incarnation involved a sharing of that rootedness. And so we learn that the material is not alien to the spiritual. Rather it is the vehicle and medium of spiritual presence and encounter. The

incarnation teaches us to view the physical world sacramentally.

We already know that sacraments are part of the very life of Christianity; the spiritual presence and power of the risen Christ are mediated to us in and through such earthy things as bread and wine. But the sacramental principle goes much further than that. Listen to these words of Teilhard de Chardin from his *Mass on the World*.

'Rich with the sap of the world, I rise up towards the Spirit whose vesture is the magnificence of the material universe but who smiles at me far beyond all victories; and, lost in the mystery of the flesh of God, I cannot tell which is the more radiant bliss, to have found the Word and so be able to achieve the mastery of matter, or to have mastered matter and so be able to attain and submit to the light of God.'

So we learn through incarnational religion both to value the material world and to view the world sacramentally as the medium of the spirit. We are not interested in flight from the world into a detached dimension of the spirit.

3 *The pattern of Christian ministry*
Then, secondly, it follows from the doctrine of the incarnation that the work of Christian ministry – in which we all share – must be patterned on the mission of the Son of God. Just as he emptied himself and came among us not to be served but to serve, and just as he involved himself in the ordinary day to day life of the people, their joys and sorrows, fears and hopes, eating with publicans and sinners, drawing on everyday life for his teaching in parables, putting himself at risk by his involvement in the world, and eventually suffering a cruel death rather than withdrawing or escaping from involvement in the world, however hostile, just so should we involve ourselves in the life, the cares and the joys of those around us. We see such Christian involvement and service take heroic forms in the saints like Mother Teresa in Calcutta, or those who devote their lives, say to medical

mission, living among the people they serve, and sometimes dying of the disease they came to cure. But we also see the same fundamental qualities and attitudes, modelled on the incarnate one, in less exalted forms, in all Christian ministry, which does not hold aloof in a private churchy or pietistic world, but shares the lives of people in a local community, making itself available to people in their need, whether to rejoice or to mourn.

We see the same spirit in St Paul, of course, who declared that he would be all things to all men, in order to win some for Christ; and I think of many dedicated parish priests and lay folk up in Lancashire where I was a curate, who threw themselves into the life of the local community, often making themselves very vulnerable, but giving their time and energy and care to others, young and old and in between.

So the second thing that follows from the doctrine of the incarnation is a pattern of Christian ministry.

'Then he poured water into a basin, and began to wash the disciples' feet, and to wipe them with the towel with which he was girded. . . .' 'When he had washed their feet and taken his garments, and resumed his place, he said to them, "Do you know what I have done to you? You call me Teacher and Lord, and you are right, for so I am. If I, then, your Lord and Teacher have washed your feet, you also ought to wash one another's feet. For I have given you an example, that you also should do as I have done to you." '

4 *The social gospel*
But there is a third consequence of the doctrine, which needs to be brought out. The presence of God in the midst of our world does not only mean that we must value the material structures of creation and the personal structures of human existence; it also means that we must value and take seriously and concern ourselves with the communal and political structures of human life.

'My kingdom is not of this world.' That does not mean that

14

Jesus is only concerned with an other-worldly spiritual realm. That is a total misinterpretation. It means that the authority of Jesus over this world is God's authority, not the authority of a human king. But the gospel of the incarnation entails that God's authority is to take effect and exercise control precisely in this world, not only in the hearts of individual men, but in every facet of their life, physical (and that means economic) and inter-personal (and that means social and political – not just our face-to-face dealings with our neighbour). The kingdom of God is a powerful symbol for the realization of God's will on earth in just and equal conditions, as well as in men's hearts.

Thus it follows from the incarnation that Christian disciples cannot rest content with unjust and oppressive conditions, with the increasing gap between rich and poor nations, with the deprivation of the rights of the majority by the minority on racial grounds, with the abuse of state power over the consciences of men and women. The World Council of Churches is right to concern itself with these matters, and there is an authentic Christian voice in men like Alan Paton and Alexander Solzhenitsyn, who have protested and go on protesting against radical evil in human affairs.

Of course there is a problem here about the methods to be used to right these wrongs. For while there can be no doubt that it follows from the doctrine of the incarnation that we should in Jesus' name take steps to right these wrongs, it also follows from the example of our Lord that there are distinctively Christian ways of confronting the world's evil. The way of incarnation, it seems, when it runs foul of earthly power, becomes the way of the cross. I do not myself believe that we can deduce from this fundamental Christian truth that, for example, the use of force is never justified. On the contrary, to abstract oneself from situations where the use of force may be the only course of action that one can conscientiously take would be to go flat against this incarnation principle which we have been exploring. I remember reading a book on the prevention of war which trenchantly argued that the way of pacifism is in fact the way of Pilate washing his hands of a matter which he knew he ought to act on. And yet, I see in Jesus Christ and the way of the cross a radical alternative to the vicious circle of violence and counterviolence in which men and nations get so easily entrapped. Well, these are fearfully difficult questions, much too difficult to solve tonight. But an incarnational religion plunges us right into such questions and refuses to escape the sort of agonizings that I have just been touching on about the use or renunciation of force.

I have argued that three things follow from the doctrine of the incarnation: one, we are to value the material world in which the Word was made flesh; two, we are to follow the example of our Lord, who went about with publicans and sinners and taught his disciples to love and serve their fellow men; three, we cannot abstract ourselves from concern with politics, agonizing though the choices may be. And of course, the resources of incarnational religion are those of the risen Christ himself who gives himself to us today in bread and wine. He alone enables the disciple (and the student of divinity) to follow his own instruction.

4

PASSIONTIDE

We are now in the season known as Passiontide, and we are approaching Holy Week, when we meditate upon the central mystery of Christianity – the fact that when God in the person of his son came to share our human life and make himself known to us in the closest and most personal way possible – in an actual human life – men put him to death on a trumped-up charge. Certainly many people acclaimed him. Hosanna to the Son of David, they shouted, strewing his path with palm branches on the first Palm Sunday. But before the week was out, he was nailed to the cross, betrayed and deserted even by his friends.

In two weeks' time, of course, we shall be celebrating the resurrection and the power of God over death and the worst that men can do. The story did not end on the cross. But our Christian faith cannot be all resurrection. We cannot by-pass the cross, moving straight to Easter. Just as Jesus had to endure the cross, we must be prepared to stay with him, and be with him in his passion and his cross, just as we know he is with us, whatever the world may do to us.

We must, that is, be realistic. Our great temptation is to be unrealistic. Most of us, these days in this part of the world, do not bear the mark of the cross. Our kind of life is designed to conceal the realities of suffering, despair and death, as much as possible. I suspect that, in our heart of hearts, many of us want a Christianity without the cross.

1 *Christian realism*

Several years ago now, in one of the Sunday papers, there was an article entitled, 'Why must Christians be so miserable?' The writer took great exception to the view of the world summed up by the words of the old burial service: 'We give thee thanks for that it hath pleased thee to deliver this our brother out of the miseries of this sinful world. . .'. He told how the gloomy atmosphere of church oppressed him as a child. For him the world was not miserable, but was beautiful and exciting. The people he knew were on the whole kindly and good; the concept of all-pervading sinfulness made no sense. He went on a little later: 'If there is a God, then surely he must manifest himself in lovely things, in the primrose and the poem; the leaping salmon and the galloping horse; in girls, wine, butterflies, buttercups, swift waters, sunset skies,

in Beethoven and Shakespeare; above all in the human spirit
– its tenderness in love, its imagination and its daring, its
courage before death.'

All one's instincts are to agree with that. I think we do not
want to interpret our faith very much in terms of the glory
and wonder of God and his creation. We want to be shouting
'Hosanna', as they did the first Palm Sunday. We want an
outward-looking, positive, optimistic, dynamic Christianity
– an attractive Christianity – a Christianity which is all
resurrection. We want to forget that you cannot have
resurrection without first a death.

Certainly the burial service in the old prayer book version
does contain a pretty jaundiced view of the world. But I
wonder whether that journalist's view is any less one-sided.
The world is indeed beautiful and exciting, but what about
the devastation of earthquake, fire and flood, famine and
plague? We cannot just shut our eyes to the facts of madness
and disease. And is it true to say that people on the whole are
kindly and good? I say nothing here of war and terrorism.
But we are only too well aware that ordinary people – people
like those who surrounded that writer's childhood with
kindness and goodness – in a situation of racial tension, say,
or community violence, are just as capable of reacting
viciously and callously as was the crowd that shouted
'crucify'. The world is full of the most marvellous and joyful
possibilities; but it is also full of the most terrible ones; and
there can be no profound view of the world which ignores one
or other of these sides to it. And a Christianity without the
cross cannot even begin to face up to the dark side.

After all, the Christian religion is not just an optimistic
way of looking at things. If it were, it would only work for
people who are all right anyway – people who have had a
secure childhood, people who are blessed with a happy and
pleasant nature, people whose life is pretty comfortable.
Whereas the real strength of Christianity lies in the power it
gives men and women to overcome the most unhappy and

disastrous circumstances – in its power to change people's lives, to enable men to face and to transcend the worst the world can do. The spiritual resources given us in Christian faith are only seen to be real and powerful when they are tested and not found illusory, when Christian love is experienced not as a vague and woolly idea – but as something very costly, something triumphing against heavy odds, something which sustains and upholds a man, no matter what he may be going through.

2 *The cost of forgiveness*
And so we are brought back to the figure bowed to the ground, overcome with horror and dismay in the garden of Gethsemane – to the broken figure on the cross, crying out, 'My God, my God, why hast thou forsaken me?' The extraordinary thing about Christian faith is that it is there that we are asked to discern the supreme revelation of our God; to realize that these are the lengths to which he is prepared to go to win us back to him. Christian piety has seen many things in the cross of Christ. We can see a new way of overcoming the world's evil; we can see the cost of the divine forgiveness and the divine love; we can see the eternal Son of God, through whom the worlds were made, accepting responsibility for the evil in the world, bearing the brunt of it, offering himself as a target for all our conscious and unconscious aggression. And in all this we can recognize the possibility of reconciliation – that our sin is not an ultimate barrier between ourselves and God, that God accepts us irrespective of the consequences to himself of accepting us as we are. And of course, recognition of that acceptance, accepting that we are accepted, as Paul Tillich puts it, is the starting point for change and renewal as the love of God takes root in us.

> When I survey the wondrous cross
> On which the Prince of glory died,
> My richest gain I count but loss,
> And pour contempt on all my pride.

Then there is that other wonderful hymn which we sing at Passiontide:

> My song is love unknown,
> My Saviour's love to me,
> Love to the loveless shown,
> That they might lovely be.

And incidentally I would take those lines – 'love to the loveless shown that they might lovely be' – as an answer to that writer in the Sunday paper, when he says that God, if there is a God must manifest himself in lovely things. God does manifest himself in lovely things, but he does more than that. He manifests himself to the loveless that *they* might lovely be. In other words he transforms the loveless into the lovely – he's not just concerned with what is lovely already. The hymn goes on:

> O who am I,
> That for my sake
> My Lord should take
> Frail flesh and die?

> Here might I stay and sing,
> No story so divine;
> Never was love, dear King,
> Never was grief like thine!
> This is my Friend,
> In whose sweet praise
> I all my days
> Could gladly spend.

3 *A new kind of life*

But obviously this kind of response will not do by itself. The passive contemplation of the cross of Christ is no good as a permanent occupation. I cannot really stay here and sing. I cannot really spend all my days in his sweet praise. These hymns certainly bring out the wonder of God's love – love to the loveless shown that they might lovely be – and express most movingly, the response of gratitude it evokes. But there's more to Passiontide than that.

> Were the whole realm of nature mine,
> That were an offering far too small;
> Love so amazing, so divine,
> Demands my soul, my life, my all.

The events of Passiontide and Holy Week are not simply for our contemplation and our gratitude. They make possible for us a new kind of life. You see, when Christians speak of death and resurrection, or of a new life – a new creation, or of finding one's life through losing it, either they're just paying lip service to a received scheme of ideas entitled 'the way of the cross', or they are speaking from experience of a discovery they have made – that this really is the way things work at the profoundest level, that this paradox of life throught death reflects the basic truth about our existence.

This really is how love works. This kind of utterly self-giving love lies at the heart of things; for it is our God who loves like that. It is our God whom we see most clearly in that head-hung figure on the Cross. Our Indian friends often compare Christianity's central symbols of the cross unfavourably with their image of the God, Siva, dancing the world into being. Well the love of God is seen in creation, but not only there. It is also, and most especially seen in the lengths God is prepared to go to bring about our redemption. And so, if we mean what we say when we sing, 'love so amazing, so divine, demands my soul, my life, my all', then we are acknowledging the claim of this way of the cross on us – and not only the claim, but also the power of ultimate self-giving love to change the world.

I find that there is more in this kind of response to life than simply perceiving God in the primrose and the poem, the leaping salmon and the galloping horse, in girls, wine,

21

butterflies, buttercups, swift waters, sunset skies, in Beethoven and Shakespeare – however true it is that he is manifest in these lovely things.

5

RESURRECTION

Rise heart; thy Lord is risen. Sing his praise
Without delayes,
Who takes thee by the hand, that thou likewise
With him mayst rise
That as his death calcined thee to dust
His life may make thee gold, and much more, just.

George Herbert's 'Easter' poem speaks of the joy of the Christian at the resurrection of his Lord. The poem rightly reminds us of Good Friday – there can be no resurrection without first a death. And it speaks too of the effect of Christ's resurrection on us: the risen Christ, it suggests, with its imagery from alchemy, is to transform us utterly. This is no easy transformation. We are to share not simply Christ's resurrection, but rather his death and resurrection. We are first to be pulverized – calcined into dust – before we are changed, transformed to gold. And, adds Herbert, this dust-to-gold transformation is to be given ethical cash-value. We are to be made just.

1 *Participation in Christ's death and resurrection*
We should, I think, be clear in our minds that talk of the Christian's participation in Christ's death and resurrection has a double meaning. It has a literal meaning and a

22

metaphorical one. The poet concentrates on the latter – the metaphorical sense – the sense in which we are to die to sin and selfishness and rise to a new transformed life, life for others, a spirit-filled life. For the poet is perfectly well aware that this moral and spiritual transformation cannot be our own work. It is rather the work of the Spirit of the living Christ. Our new song will achieve its harmony only if the Spirit resolves our vying dissonances, as we learn from the third stanza of the poem:

> Consort both heart and lute, and twist a song
> Pleasant and long;
> Or since all musick is but three parts vied
> And multiplied;
> O let thy blessed Spirit bear a part
> And make up our defects with his sweet art.

But Christians speak not only of a moral and spiritual transformation, of being made by the Spirit to share (in this metaphorical sense) in Christ's death and resurrection. They speak also, quite literally, of resurrection from the dead. The resurrection of Christ from the dead, however elusive and mysterious, was a real event. It was not a resuscitation. Christ was raised in a new mode of being to God's right hand. But this resurrection left real traces in our world – an empty tomb, and, perhaps, a shroud. I do not know about that and in any case it is better to stick to the words of the risen Christ according to St John: Blessed are they who have not seen and yet have believed.

More importantly, the fact that Christ was alive after his death was shown to his disciples. And in a different way Christians down the ages have known that their Lord is a living Lord. We ourselves encounter him here and now in his spiritual and sacramental presence in the Eucharist. Moreover, Christians believe that death is not the end for any man or woman created in the image of God. We too shall live. We await in hope another transformation from dust to gold. This is to speak of the literal sense in which we hope to share in Christ's death and resurrection. A real death – we shall indeed die – and a real resurrection – by the power and love of God we shall indeed be raised. Christians see Christ's resurrection as the anticipation, the first fruits, the foretaste, of God's ultimate purpose to raise the dead, transformed, for eternity.

2 *A future beyond death*

Obviously all this is nonsense if we do not believe in God. But if we do believe in God, let us take our belief seriously and accept its implications, that this present life is not all there is, and further that God has given us, in the resurrection of Jesus Christ from the dead, a token, not only of present communion with a living Lord, but of future resurrection for us all.

One of the results of the Christian/Marxist dialogues of the nineteen-sixties was recognition that the Marxists' hope for future transformation comes unstuck precisely over the question of death. The dedicated Marxist can have no hope of participation in the classless society of the future – his utopia is in any case always receding beyond the horizon. But for Christian faith, the poor and the unloved of every generation will themselves be transformed and given a share in Christ's resurrection.

The two senses of sharing in Christ's death and resurrection are, of course, linked. It is the same Lord, who rose from the dead that first Easter Sunday morning and with whom we shall be raised in the last day, who, by his Spirit, begins our moral and spiritual transformation now, and who, by his Spirit, begins to make us and our world more just. We do not have to wait until we die to experience the power of the resurrection. It is manifest already in changed lives, in astonishing human goodness in face of intolerable evil, and in all the manifestations of renewal and care and love, including the struggle for human justice in our times. For, as

George Herbert saw, the gold of a transformed life and a risen heart is, much more, a matter of becoming just.

3 The world's need for resurrection

God knows we need resurrection and the world needs resurrection. I remember one Good Friday finishing reading the last of Solzhenitsyn's volumes on the Gulag Archipelago – his indictment of the monumental injustices of Soviet power in the system of prison camps and forced labour throughout the Soviet Union. Our century is truly a terrible one – millions of people crucified by the abuse of unrestrained power. But the sources of transformation and resurrection are here in the Spirit of the living God and of the risen Christ. We can glimpse this in the phenomenon of Solzhenitsyn himself, and in some of the stories he tells of human courage and goodness in the midst of so much evil. And we must look for such signs of resurrection in people and in politics today. We look for them in our distracted and suffering world and in our own country and in ourselves.

If we are realists, we know we cannot change from dust to gold and our society cannot change from dust to gold by our own efforts in the spheres of morals and politics, any more than in the literal case of rising from the dead. Resurrection is always God's act. We are only instruments in his hands, and in the end, in death, we have to yield ourselves wholly into his hands.

But the Easter message is one of hope. Christ is risen and he shares his risen life with you and with me.

> Rise heart; thy Lord is risen. . . .

May he indeed take us by the hand, that we with him may rise, that as his death calcined us to dust, his life may make us gold, and, much more, just. Amen.

25

6

THE ASCENSION

We Christians have a double task in God's world. We have, on the one hand, to let ourselves, more and more, become the vehicles and channels of God's love in transforming the world (and, of course, to let ourselves in the process be transformed more and more by that love) and, on the other hand, we have the task of bearing witness to the reality and truth of God as the God of grace, the God of forgiving, self-sacrificial love.

1 *The importance of doctrine*
There is a tendency nowadays in the Church to concentrate on the former task, the task of transformation, to the neglect of the latter, the task of witness. But that is to forget the fundamental Christian fact, that the truths to which we are called to bear witness are the very source of the transforming power by which, as instruments in God's hands and as living members in Christ's body, we are to play our part in the realization of God's loving purposes on earth. If we neglect the truths to which our action is and can only be a response, we will, as sure as night follows day, get snarled up in the self-defeating structures of the do-gooder, or else get caught in the web of some secular ideology, with its inevitable abuse of power. On the contrary, our work for peace and justice and human brotherhood and for the care of people must and can only be done in the name and power of the God of the cross, the God of unlimited self-sacrificial love.

So I make no apology for talking to you this evening about Christian truth rather than Christian practice, and in fact I am going to say something about the ascension.

But having, by way of preamble, defended this plan to talk

about Christian truth, I find I must launch into a second preamble; for there is a problem about Christian truth today. Christians notoriously disagree about it. Anyone who has read the report of the Church of England Doctrine Commission, entitled *Christian Believing* (SPCK), will be only too aware that there exists a deep divide among Christian thinkers. On one hand there are those who see the place of divine revelation as being located in certain specific events in history, the events celebrated traditionally at the great Christian festivals of Christmas, Good Friday, Easter and Ascension, events to which the Church's faith bears witness and her practice responds. On the other hand there are those who see the place of divine revelation as being located rather in the developing tradition and practice of the Church herself, as, by God's Spirit, she is fashioned into the instrument of his saving love in every age and generation. This is a big divide. There is a sense in which we have to learn to live with it (and the *Christian Believing* report was a helpful statement of how to do so); but if we believe, as I do, that the first alternative is right, we cannot just *assume* that those who disagree with us are wrong. We have to argue the case for what we think we have seen of God's own self-involvement in the creation through the incarnation, crucifixion and exaltation of his Son.

2 *The meaning of the doctrine of the Ascension*

My remarks on the ascension, then, are to be taken as part of that enterprise – the exploration and defence of Christian truth. It is a difficult part. Of all the great festivals, Ascension Day is the least immediately revealing and significant for us. We can perhaps appreciate the wonder and the force of the incarnation, of God the Son coming amongst us to share our joys and sorrows and to reveal his love in human form, taking personal responsibility for the world's ills and bearing the brunt of them himself. The resurrection, too, however hard we may find it to believe, makes clear and simple sense as the

27

vindication of Christ's life and way, and as God's triumph over sin and death. We can readily see in the resurrection of Jesus Christ from the dead the foretaste and promise of God's ultimate destiny for his redeemed creation. But what of the ascension? What do these elusive stories of the risen Christ being taken up into heaven really mean? What is being symbolized by the crude pictures of Christian art down the centuries which show the disciples staring up at the feet of the ascending Christ disappearing into a cloud? If anything calls out for demythologization, surely it is this.

Well, yes; but we must not immediately suppose that what is being symbolized is some this-worldly, purely moral truth. We have to reckon with the possibility that these stories and myths and pictures seek to represent to us some genuinely transcendent, genuinely supernatural fact, which strains to breaking-point the powers of human language and representation, as they endeavour to carry our minds over into some apprehension, however imperfect, of the act of God in the exaltation of Jesus. This would be to claim that the ascension rounds off the great sequence of saving events which is the heart of the Christian Gospel. Of course there is more to come; there is the outpouring of the Spirit at Pentecost and the ongoing life of the Church, the Body of Christ, the instrument of God's transforming power about which I spoke at the beginning. But the ascension marks the end of that crucial period of extra-special divine presence and self-revelation which we call the incarnation.

Although the risen Christ was manifested to the disciples in visible and apparently tangible form, that was only a foretaste of the ultimate resurrection. It was specifically not the mode of his presence and activity in the Church and in the world of our present experience. The one who, in Karl Barth's phrase, had journeyed into a far country to make himself known to us and to win our love, must return, must come home to the Father, before his coming again, universally, no longer restricted to a particular slice of space and time and history, in the spiritual and sacramental forms which we know today. The ascension marks this decisive break. The revealing events have happened. Now begins the new time of the Church's witness by word and deed, empowered by the risen Christ, yes, but in his spiritual and sacramental modes of presence and activity.

There is one further thing of which the ascension speaks to us. It speaks to us of the permanent taking of our humanity into God – again a foretaste of God's ultimate future for his creation. We are not, of course, really to suppose that God the Son left the Father's side during the incarnation. Even in the cry of dereliction on the cross we cannot suppose the blessed Trinity to be split up. These things took place in eternity in the heart of God even as they were lived out in time in agony and bloody sweat. But equally we must suppose that the eternal love of the Son for the Father is newly and permanently expressed through the humanity of Jesus exalted, as we pictorially say, to God's right hand. And there we shall join him. That is the promise of the resurrection. (I think our Eastern Orthodox brothers go too far in speaking of our eventual divinization. Our humanity will doubtless be transformed as Jesus' humanity was but in neither case can we really suppose that it ceases to be humanity, created personal being.)

Well, these are some of the things of which the ascension speaks to us. And I think we should mull over these things. How else can we hope to show that Christian faith and practice are a response and witness to real acts of God in human history.

3 *The difference made by these doctrines*
To conclude, let us go back to the practical side, the side I set aside in order to talk theology. For one of the big questions that arises out of that dispute between Christian thinkers over the place of revelation (so clearly evidenced in *Christian Believing*) is whether such doctrinal disputes have practical

consequences. Does it make any difference to our life as committed Christian men and women whether we believe that God himself, without ceasing to be God, in the person of his Son, took our nature upon him and came among us, dying a cruel death and being raised and exalted again, in his humanity, to God's right hand? Does it matter whether we believe this? Are not the qualities of life which Christianity commends, love, forgiveness, acceptance, self-sacrifice, community, just the same, with or without all this theology?

Well, I suppose the proof of the pudding lies in the eating. But I can only say that I think it does matter. To put the matter very simply: I, for one, find inspiration, not just in the recommendation coming to me out of the Christian tradition, of a certain style of life, but in the fact that my Lord and God actually trod this path for me.

> My song is love unknown,
> My Saviour's love for me,
> Love to the loveless shown,
> That they might lovely be.

The one who sits at God's right hand is the one whose story is in the Gospel. We do not pray to an unknown God. He is unknown no longer. Moreover this is the one who comes to meet us still in the Spirit and in the bread and the wine, the one who actually sustains us and inspires us in whatever form of Christian life and love we let him create in us. And this is the one who has gone before us to prepare a place for us.

It is because I think all of this theology is true that I have presented it to you this Ascensiontide.

7

PENTECOST

Whitsunday is rather different from the other great festivals of the Christian Church. Christmas, Good Friday, Easter and Ascension are all explicitly to do with Jesus Christ, the incarnate Son of God who came to the world at a particular point in history to make God known to us, and to win us back to God by his own unlimited, self-sacrificial love. Now it is this concrete, particular, personal presence of God as an actual human life, which we read about in the Gospels, that enables Christian men and women to know who God is, what he is like and what his purpose and will for us and for the world are. That is the point of the incarnation. We see God in the face of Jesus Christ – even headhung on the Cross, as well as in his risen glory. That is the special claim of Christianity, that he who has seen Christ has seen the Father. It gives our faith in God a particular personal form and content. The God of the Christians is not a vague, mysterious, hidden power. Of course there is a sense in which God remains mysterious, incomprehensible and hidden, even in his revelation. But there is also this quite specific sense in which he has made himself known and knowable in Jesus Christ.

1 *God's self-revelation, past and present*
But the events of which Christmas, Good Friday and Easter speak are in the past, nearly two thousand years ago, and the ascension of Christ, although we believe he lives and reigns and has taken our humanity permanently into God, nevertheless marked the end of that particular historical self-manifestation of God to man in time. It had to be a particular historical series of events, if the human life in which God came to us was to be real and genuinely human. Like all

31

human lives it was located at a particular place and time and as such is receding further and further into the past. That cannot be the whole story. Christians do not simply remember a more and more distant person and sequence of events, however significant. Rather they experience the living spiritual reality of God present and active in their lives today. The God who made himself known in a life lived and a death died at a particular place long ago, relates himself to us here and now in the present and at all times by his Spirit. This is what we celebrate on Whitsunday – the gift of the Spirit, here, now, always. This is why the risen Christ had to go away – that unique temporal revelation was at an end – so that he might come again in the Spirit, unrestricted by time and place.

But, again, we have to remember that it is precisely because he did come then in such a particular concrete tangible human form that we really can say that we know who he is. This is why we can equally well speak of the Spirit of Christ as of the Spirit of God. Our knowledge of God and our present relation to God are certainly in the Spirit. We do not confront Christ in the flesh as Peter and James and John did. But the spiritual relation in which we stand is given form and precision and real content just because the Spirit in us is indeed the Spirit of Christ, the Spirit of God incarnate.

Without the incarnation, experience of God in the Spirit would be extremely vague. I do not want to disparage other religions, and I think Christians are simply mistaken if they just write off what God has done and does in and through the whole religious and ethical life of man all over the world – though one cannot ignore the corruptions and distortions of religion (including those of Christianity). But I am bound to say that the kind of experience of God which comes through mysticism and yoga or the manifold symbolism of other faiths, however profound, lacks the full force of the personal and moral self-revelation of God in the incarnation and cross of his Son. As the Epistle to the Hebrews says: 'In many and

32

various ways God spoke of old to our fathers by the prophets, but in these last days he has spoken to us by a Son. . . .'

So when we sing at Passiontide, 'My song is love unknown . . .' we mean that it used to be unknown, but it is now known, personally, in the one who, out of love, came among us and loved us to the end. And the Holy Spirit at work in the Church today is not a vague mystical presence or unknown irrational force, but the Spirit of the living Christ, leading us into the truth of God.

2 *Trinitarian faith*

Christian talk of the Spirit, I have been urging, is talk of God present and active in us, in the Church and in the world. It is talk of the same God who in the person of Christ, made himself humanly present and knowable as the one who walked the hills of Galilee and died on a cross outside Jerusalem nearly two thousand years ago. This understanding of God as the God who comes to us both in the person of his Son and in the person of his Spirit is summed up in the doctrine of the Trinity which reflects the central Christian recognition that God *is* Love, that he does not depend on us to love, but is in himself love given and love received. We see that most clearly in the relation of the incarnate Son to his heavenly Father. This, we believe, mirrors the eternal love of God the Father and God the Son. But we see it too in Christian experience of the Spirit, as in that extraordinary passage in Romans 8, verses 26 to 28.

'Likewise the Spirit helps us in our weakness. For we do not know how to pray as we ought, but the Spirit himself intercedes for us with sighs too deep for words! And he who searches the hearts of men knows what is in the mind of the Spirit because the Spirit intercedes for the saints according to the will of God. We know that in everything God works for good with those who love him, who are called according to his purpose.'

There is expressed here a sense that in our feeble prayers

and worship we arc caught up into God's own interior dialogue. So it is not only the incarnation that reveals the internal love of God, on the analogy of a father's love for his son, but also the gift of the Spirit, by which we too are taken into the trinitarian life of God. I think it is important that we should realize that the living God is much more rich and complex in his inner being and relations than the analogy of a single isolated person might suggest. We do not relate to God as we relate to another human being over against us externally. God *is* God over against us as the transcendent source of our being. But he is also God within us, taking up our intercessions into his, and we ought to think of our worship and our life as Christians as being caught up into the internally differentiated life of God. Our life and our destiny as Christians lie *in* God.

3 *The Spirit of Jesus Christ*

Now our reflections on the meaning of Whitsunday have taken us far into the deep complexities of the Christian doctrine of God, and before we get out of our depth we must come back – as Christians always must come back – to take our bearings again from the revelation of God in Jesus Christ. Just because the Spirit of whom we have been speaking is the Spirit of the living God who was revealed in Christ and indeed is also to be thought of as the Spirit of Christ – the Spirit, that is, who proceedeth from the Father and the Son (if we may risk offending our Eastern Orthodox brethren by insisting on the '*filioque*' clause) – just because the spirit is the Spirit of Christ, we *must* think of and experience our relation to God as something thoroughly personal and focused on Christ the human face of God.

This means that we ought not to get carried away by talk or even experience of so-called charismatic gifts which are impersonal, irrational or divisive. We know that God is not like that, simply because of Jesus Christ. We ought, as St Paul says, to test the spirits. The charismatic movement in

34

the Christian Churches is a striking phenomenon and it is fine if it awakens us to a new sense of the power of God that makes for love, joy, peace and fellowship, and inspires us, in the Church, to work for a more just and humane world. But it is no use whatsoever if it fosters irrationalism and divisiveness in the Church. 'By their fruits ye shall know them.'

I cannot resist quoting Austin Farrer's marvellous sermon on 'Inspiration by the Spirit' at this point: 'The trouble about an indiscreet belief in inspiration is that it smothers reason. A man who declares, "This is what the Spirit directs", is not required to give a reason; surely God does not argue his cases. But I say to you, always suspect claims to inspired guidance which bypass reasoned argument. There are not fewer reasons for what God ordains than for other things; there are more, far more. There are all the reasons in the world, if we can but find them. For is not he wise?'

So let us pray for this Spirit of the living God to come upon us and take us into God, in the words of the collects for the Sunday after Ascension Day and for Whitsunday, which I shall conflate together.

> O God the King of glory, who hast exalted thine only Son, Jesus Christ, with great triumph unto thy kingdom in heaven, we beseech thee leave us not comfortless; but send to us thy Holy Spirit to comfort us and exalt us into the same place whither our Saviour Christ is gone before, and grant us by the same Spirit to have a right judgement in all things – through the merits of Christ Jesus our Saviour, who liveth and reigneth with thee in the unity of the same Spirit, one God, world without end. Amen.

8

THE TRINITY

The question I want us to think about this Trinity Sunday is this: what is the difference between the Old Testament understanding of God, a fine example of which we heard from Isaiah 40 as our first lesson, and the Christian understanding of God, which we see beginning to form in passages like our second lesson from 1 Peter – 'Blessed be the God and Father of our Lord Jesus Christ' – and which is summed up, perhaps a little drily, in the doctrine of the Trinity? Not that the 1 Peter passage is in any way dry. The words, so magnificently set to music by S.S. Wesley in his famous anthem, express a great sense of religious exaltation, a rich understanding of God, and a full and heartfelt response to the God revealed to us in Christ and the Spirit. If we are to begin to do justice to Christian trinitarian belief, we have to realize that is what the doctrine of the Trinity is about, namely the richness and the wonder of the living God, whose action in incarnation and inspiration creates this profound and exalted response of trinitarian faith, both in worship and by participation.

1 *A monotheistic religion*
What is the difference, then, between the God of Isaiah 40 and the God of the Christians? It is a very difficult question to handle fairly. For one thing the universal monotheism of Isaiah 40-45 is only one strand in the complex development of Israel's faith and the 1 Peter passage is only one example of the early Christians' enriched response to God's self-revelation in Christ and the Spirit. Nor should I have slipped from talking about the difference between the Old Testament understanding of God and the Christian understanding of

36

God into talking about the difference between the God of Isaiah 40 and the God of the Christians. For our starting point must surely be that in reality they are the same God. The God of Israel *is* the God and Father of our Lord Jesus Christ and thus the God of the Christians.

One of the difficulties of trying to explain and commend trinitarian belief is that one tends in doing so to disparage other men's understanding of God. I shall be arguing at the end that we should not do that where other world faiths such as Hinduism, Sikhism and Islam are concerned, but least of all should we cut off Christian belief in God from Jewish belief. For the faith of Israel is the root and trunk from which Christian trinitarian belief flowered out, and we go hopelessly astray if we think that the full flowering of trinitarian belief enables us to dispense with Jewish monotheism. Not at all. The author of the letter to the Hebrews was absolutely right, when he began his letter like this: 'In many and various ways God spoke of old to our fathers by the prophets; but in these last days he has spoken to us by a Son, whom he appointed heir of all things, through whom he created the world.' The subject of that sentence, the one who spoke first through the prophets and then through the Son, undoubtedly is one and the same.

Well, we have not got very far with my question: what is the difference? Let us think first about Israel's faith in God. We can trace through the Old Testament something of the development from what has been called the 'henotheism' of the early days, where Jahweh was thought of as this people's God, a jealous God, more powerful than the gods of other folk, but still in essence a tribal God, right through to the universal monotheism of the later prophets and psalms (and of course of Genesis 1 – a late work) where God is the God of the whole earth, creator of all men.

A number of features stand out as peculiarly significant in this developing faith. First, the moral rigorism of Jewish faith. God demands high standards of ethical conduct, as well as undeviating loyalty. Secondly, the personal and moral nature of God himself. He may appear a somewhat fierce figure in the early days. But he came to be thought of as supremely characterized by steadfast love; he grieves over his chosen people's waywardness, and promises that, come what may, he will not forsake them. Thirdly, we may note that Israel's God is the lord of history. In his providence he selects a chosen people and fashions their response over centuries of external and internal struggle. Their calling is to be a light to the nations. They are to look to the future, to await the day of the Lord, when Israel will be vindicated and God's purposes for all men fulfilled.

This ethical monotheism contained many profound strands of religious experience – wonder at God's creation, a sense of the meaningfulness of history and the world as moving toward a destiny and a goal under God, a sense of God as Father to his people, a sense of awe at the holiness of God (witness first Isaiah's vision in the Temple), a sense too of the dynamics of guilt and forgiveness, trust in God and gratitude (think of the psalms), a sense of the resources of God for human living. 'They who wait for the Lord shall renew their strength, they shall mount up with wings like eagles, they shall run and not be weary, they shall walk and not faint.'

2 Beyond monotheism

But there are problems, even with such a sublime religious faith as this. I am not thinking here of the tendencies towards legalism in later Judaism, nor of the problems created by the restriction of this consciousness of God to a particular people. Certainly the young Christian Church made an extraordinarily rapid break with Judaism on both these scores, with a Gospel of reconciliation preached to Jew and gentile alike. But what I am really thinking of are certain tendencies, discernible in any such sublime ethical monotheism – the tendency to magnify God at the expense of man ('It

38

is he who sits above the circle of the earth, and its inhabitants are like grasshoppers') – in other words, the tendency – I stress the word 'tendency' – towards emphasizing the remoteness and otherness of God.

Then there is the failure really to meet the problem of evil. Ancient Israel was most profoundly conscious of it, yes (think of Job); but, despite the intimations of the idea of redemptive suffering in the Suffering Servant passages of second Isaiah, she had no real way of coping with the fact of innocent suffering in a world for which God is ultimately responsible. Then there is another problem. To think of God in personal terms is inevitably to think of him in relation. Persons exist in relation to one another. And certainly the God of Israel *is* thought of throughout the Old Testament as being the God *of* his people; he is constantly portrayed in relation to Adam, to the patriarchs, the kings and the prophets and to all who turn to him for succour. But there is something of an *impasse* when we think of such a God as he is in himself. Can we really suppose that his personal being depends on his relation to his creatures and his people?

In Christian belief, this same God is thought of in a new way, simply as a result of the events concerning Jesus Christ, his cross, his resurrection and its aftermath. It is no longer possible to separate God from man, way up there above the circle of the earth; for God, without ceasing to be God, has made himself present and known here in our midst. In Jesus we see the human face of God. Moreover, we see in the cross of Christ God's making himself vulnerable to the world's ills – not just sympathizing – but bearing the brunt of it himself, accepting responsibility for evil and suffering and taking it upon himself. And as we reflect on what God must be like to be able, without ceasing to be God, to live out that human life and relate himself to himself in the manner in which we read of Jesus' prayers to the Father, we see that this relation between the Father and the incarnate Son reflects a real relation in God as he is in himself. We realize that God contains within himself the fulness of love given and received, before ever he creates a world. So for Christians, this sublime transcendent God is discovered to be Love – not just in that he loves us – but that he is already in himself the lover and the beloved.

3 *God within us*

There is also much to be said, though time prevents it now, of the way in which the God whose human face we see in Jesus comes to us in each generation by his Spirit, binding us to himself and enabling us, from within, to share, by adoption and grace, in the trinitarian life of God. We discover, in worship and in life, something of what it means to be caught up and sustained not only by, but also in, God – he in us and we in him. There is another God-God relation encountered here. The Spirit within intercedes with God 'with groans too deep for words'. We believe, too, that in God's future, all will be gathered up, through Christ and in the Spirit, into the God will be all in all.

Curiously, then, the doctrine of the Trinity safeguards the Godness of God – he *is* himself Love – *and* the humanity of God, his closeness to us by incarnation and indwelling.

Well, I can only hint at these mysteries – and I guess I only glimpse them pretty hazily in any case.

4 *Other faiths*

One final word: nothing that I have said should make us disparage the faith and spirituality of other men in other faiths. For they too, in their different ways, just like the men of Israel, have seen something of God, and we should look for signs of God's and indeed of Christ's universal presence and activity in them and their traditions. Christians are bound, I think, to say that the Spirit of God and of Christ acts there more hiddenly than in and through the incarnate life to which we, as Christians, bear a special witness. But, ultimately, we have to say that the God of the Christians is the same God as the God of the Hindus and the Sikhs and the Muslims. In speaking to them of Christ, we do not speak of a total stranger, any more then when we speak of Christ to the Jew – though maybe in our dialogue with men of other faiths we should *speak* of Christ rather less and trust him and show him rather more.

May I commend to you, this Trinity Sunday evening, the trinitarian faith of the Christians, as something that can and ought to be thought about, as well as prayed in, worshipped in and lived in.

9

THE DOCTRINE OF MAN IN THE CHRISTIAN DOCTRINE OF CREATION

At a concert in the Snape Maltings, I met a lady in the interval who, when she heard that I lectured on the philosophy of religion, asked me if I believed that animals have souls. I said, not very helpfully, that it depended on what you meant by the word 'soul', but that, while there is a sense of animal 'soul' (Aristotle's in fact) which no one ought to quarrel with, in Christian doctrine we do tend to keep the world 'soul' for the rational, personal and spiritual capacities which animals do not have and which human beings, made in the image of God, do have. This lady then told me that she had recently been on a panel discussion, defending the view that animals too are made in the image of God, not just human beings. I scratched my head and said that that was an unusual view and one that would not find support in the Christian tradition. Warming to the attack, the lady said that she supposed I had an anthropomorphic picture of God, whereas she was something of a pantheist and believed that in a way we were all part of God, animals included – and therefore we should treat them better.

1 Man in the cosmos

All this made me think about the Christian doctrine of man, and about what it is that is special about man compared with the animals. And that is what I should like us to think about this evening. I hasten to say that my theme is the doctrine of man in the Christian doctrine of creation. I am not going to talk about the fall of man. We all know that things are not well with man, either as an individual or as a society. Man needs forgiveness, reconciliation, transformation (both individual and social). Christianity has much to say about those things of course. But they are not my theme tonight. I want us to think about man in God's intention, man as God created him to be.

I suspect that there is a trace of the pantheist in many of us. Maybe that lady's remark about all things being part of God did not strike you as so very peculiar or wrong. But the fact is that in the Bible and in the Christian tradition we find ourselves encouraged to think of the whole world, including animals and human beings, not as part of God or emanations from God but rather as created out of nothing – *dependent* on God for being in being and *indwelt* by the Spirit of the living God, yes – but, for all that, something quite different from God. We are not to gloss over this basic difference between the creator and his creation. But so far there is nothing special about man. We may believe that man alone is made in the image of God, but he is a creature all the same. He shares that dependence, that contingency, that being made out of nothing, that being other than God, with the rest of creation.

The fact that the world, including man, has a reliable, God-given nature means that we can find out many facts about it, and that is what goes on in places like a university, as in both the natural and human sciences we seek to penetrate

42

the structure of things and discover their God-given nature. One of the most exciting areas of science today is that of cosmology and elementary particle physics, where something of the very basic structure of created being is uncovered and disclosed in its astonishing rationality.

For instance, did you know that modern cosmology has shown that the vast size of the universe and its specific rate of expansion are necessary conditions of the emergence of life anywhere in the universe? American physicists call this the 'anthropic principle'; for it looks as if the universe is so big just because, if it were not, life would not be possible. The argument, in brief, goes like this: living beings like ourselves can emerge in cosmic evolution only if there is a certain specific distribution of elements to form the chemical basis of life. That specific distribution can only occur if the total mass of the universe is roughly what it is; for otherwise the rate of expansion that permits this specific distribution of elements would either have been too fast or else too slow. You can read more about this in a paperback by Bernard Lovell called *In the Centre of Immensities* (Granada).

I find this a fascinating argument. It revives the old argument for design and it rebuts the old complaint that the universe is just too vast for special significance to lie in this little corner of it. For it shows that the universe is so vast, just so that such corners can appear.

Actually, despite the Americans' talk of an 'anthropic principle', we still have not said what is special about man; for animals as well – the whole living world – depend on just such conditions as we have been talking about. So what is so special about man?

2 *The image of God in man*
I have two things to say here, one, I suppose, based on reason, the other on revelation.

First, I think we must do justice to the phenomenon of man in cosmic evolution. I am not saying that man is the only valuable thing in creation and that everything else is only for the sake of man. Life in all its variety is also an astonishing phenomenon. Animal life is valuable in itself. Ecologists are right to cherish the different species. We should treat animals better – not, I think, because they are made in the image of God, but just because of what they are in all their God-given variety. But with man, we do surely reach a new level. Teilhard de Chardin was surely on to something when he spoke of the emergence with man of the 'noosphere', as he called it, of mind as new higher level in the whole creative process. For the rational, personal, interpersonal and spiritual capacities of man are something special in the universe.

I know man can and does perpetrate more horrors than any other creature – I have said that is a problem – but that fact should not close our eyes to the wonder of man's powers of thought, his ability to find out these amazing secrets of the natural universe, his creativity in art and invention, his sensibility in personal relations, his capacity to love and laugh, to sympathize and help and so on – one could spell this out at length – or for that matter his religious sense, his spiritual longings, his capacity to grow in deep spirituality. A view of the universe which sees these capacities as being of special value is not a narrowing perspective; for creation's God-given powers reach wider and greater possibilities here than anywhere else, however great the non-human values may be as well.

But the question may still nag. Are we being anthropomorphic when we think of God as personal, on the analogy of the human personal beings we ourselves are? Xenophon in ancient Greece said that if fish had gods they would be magnified fish. But no, I do not think that is right. It is not that we make God after our image; our faith is that God makes us after his own image, and that is why man is a clue to the nature of God. And that things are this way round, not the reverse, is confirmed when we turn to revelation; for Christians believe that God reveals himself to us, not in a

44

stone or a tree or an animal, but in and as a man. Stones and trees and animals and men are all creatures. But only one of these natural kinds – a man – is the point of divine incarnation; and so it is that the personal qualities of mind and will and, above all, love, are indeed the image of God – for this man, Jesus, is the perfect *ikon* of the living God. And, in Christian faith, we learn not to project ourselves on to God, but to accept God's own self-projection of himself into our midst, and to discern God's nature there in his own human face – the figure of Jesus Christ.

3 *The personality of God*
There are good reasons, then, for Christian faith's high evaluation of man as the crown and priest of creation and for thinking of God in personal terms, drawn from our experience of human persons – above all, of the man Jesus. But despite all this, it is still not true to say that we Christians think of God anthropomorphically; for just because the incarnation is a matter of God revealing himself in something *other* than himself – it matters, as I say, *which* something, namely, a man, and just because man is a creature, other than God, we learn to distinguish God from man, to think of him as personal, yes, but *not* as corporeal (bodily), limited, finite, contingent – none of these aspects of man is transferred to God. Rather we think of him as infinite, incorporeal Spirit.

We do not even think of him as *a* person; we think of him as three persons in one God; for not only does Jesus himself reveal God to us, but so does the relation between God incarnate and God the Father, and so does the relation between God the Spirit in our hearts and God the Father, the creator of all things. Christian trinitarianism is profoundly unanthropomorphic. But we do not veer off course and think of God on the analogy of less than human levels of creation such as animals and trees – without any disparagement to animals and trees, which are all part of God's good creation

45

and to be valued as such and cared for by us, who are given a special commission to name them, *use* them, yes, and care for them.

So, despite the lady in the interval, I make no apology for regarding man as the crown of creation and for what I insist is not a narrow but a broad personalized view of the universe. For the source of all things is personal – is Love – and the God who is love made us for love and for fellowship with each other and with himself. And that is why I think I am right in going on to say that man alone is destined, in God's intention, for resurrection. I stick my neck out and say that only personal being is immortalizable. We may take with us vivid memories of all the good things on the way, animals included, but I doubt if there will be cats and dogs in heaven.

Let us draw these reflections to a close by meditating on Psalm 8: 'When I consider the heavens, even the works of thy fingers, the moon and the stars which thou hast ordained, what is man, that thou art mindful of him, and son of man that thou visitest him? Thou madest him little lower than the angels, to crown him with glory and worship. Thou makest him to have dominion of the works of thy hands, and thou hast put all things in subjection under his feet – all sheep and oxen, yea and the beasts of the field – the fowls of the air and the fishes of the sea and whatsoever walketh through the paths of the seas. O Lord our Governor, how excellent is thy name in the world.'

10

ATONEMENT

Christianity is often held to be a way of life, and so of course it is, but the way of life which it commends and the kind of society which it envisages – in brief a society where God is king and a life where love prevails – are bound up with certain fundamental doctrines which Christians believe. The practical goals of love and justice and community find their inspiration in a certain context of belief, belief in the basic truths set out in the creed: belief that the world is God's good creation, that God does not leave us alone in the world, but comes to us in the person of his Son and is present to us and in us in the Spirit to make known his heart of love, to overcome what is wrong with us and with the world, to forgive and to heal, and to build up the fellowship of the sons of God, the Church, the sacramental community which is itself to be a sacrament, an outward and visible sign of the inward and spiritual presence and activity of God, as he bestows on us eternal life and makes it possible for us to share in his kingdom. And of course Christians also believe in the resurrection of the dead and the perfect future consummation of this great creative process in which we are all caught up.

I think it is a great mistake to turn one's nose up at all this doctrine and say that what matters is only the struggle for love and justice in the world. For the doctrines speak of the things that make love and justice possible in and for the world. The doctrines spell out the fundamental context in which human commitment to love and justice make some ultimate sense and they also spell out the resources which are given us for making real those practical goals of love and justice and community. So we need to ponder those doctrines.

1 *A religion of redemption*

The doctrine I want us to ponder tonight is the doctrine of the atonement. You see, Christianity does not only speak of the world as a gradual creative process from matter to life to spirit; nor does it just set before us the divine acts of creation, prophecy, incarnation, Spirit, Church, kingdom, last things. Christianity, as well as being a religion of all these things, is also and perhaps primarily a religion of redemption. It takes utterly seriously what is wrong with us and with the world; and at its heart Christianity is the story of what God did and does to come to our rescue, to overcome the world's evil, to break down creaturely resistance to the creator, and to refashion us in his own image.

Christianity does not just latch on to what is good and beautiful and lovely already in the world – though it rejoices and praises God wherever it sees such things – but it also speaks of love to the love*less* shown that *they* might lovely be, as we sing in that marvellous Passiontide hymn. That is what a religion of redemption, salvation, transformation, is about. It is about a love which enters into the depths of what is unlovely – into the depths of evil and suffering – and transforms it.

Unfortunately this great doctrine of atonement – at-one-ment – which all Christians know is about the divine forgiveness, the reconciliation of man and God and man and his neighbour and the transformation of life, both individual and social – this great doctrine has been more misunderstood and been preached more grotesquely at different times in Christian history than any other central Christian truth. It is sad to have to say this, but it really is the case not only that those outside the faith have misunderstood what the doctrine of the atonement is, but that Christians themselves have expressed it in morally offensive ways – I mean in ways which have rightly called forth moral protest.

48

2 *Misunderstandings of the Atonement*

The root of the trouble has been the tendency to construct theories of the atonement out of the great biblical images which Paul and John and the other New Testament writers use in order to express most vividly the significance of God's great acts of self-sacrificial, costly love in the incarnation and cross of Jesus – I mean images drawn from the sacrificial system of the Old Covenant (now totally superseded of course) including what is now the more or less dead language of expiation, not to mention propitiation, which is really a heathen idea. I mean also images drawn from the institution of slavery – now, thank God, a thing of the past – and its language (also somewhat dated) – the language of 'redemption' itself, of being bought with a price, and I was going to say that of 'ransom' – though I fear this has acquired a horrible new life of its own in recent years with highjacks and kidnappings. I mean also images drawn from the law court – the language of 'acquittal', 'remission of penalty' and so on. It really is no good building literal theories of the atonement out of any of this powerful imagery. That is a sure recipe for moral grotesqueness and religious confusion. No, we must hold on to the central truth that underlies this imagery, namely that God 'so loved the world that he gave his only-begotten Son that whoever believes in him should not perish but have eternal life'.

3 *The meaning of salvation*

I want to make three points about this basic gospel truth, which I hope will enable us to steer clear of the mistakes which follow from an over-literal pressing of the details of the biblical imagery.

First, we are saved not just by the death of Christ, but by the whole act of incarnation: the life and death and resurrection of Christ – and by the inworking of the Spirit of the living Christ in us, in the Church and in the world. We must not isolate the cross all by itself, although of course that central Christian symbol points to the depth and cost of the divine love.

Second, we are saved by *God*'s self-sacrificial, costly, acts of love and forgiveness. We must not drive a wedge between God and Christ, as though God is too pure and holy to get his fingers dirty in the mire of this sinful world. That idea is utterly shipwrecked on the rock of the incarnation; for Christ is God. In fact we have to go further than John 3.16 – it is not simply that God sent his Son or gave his Son. He came himself in the person of his Son – into the midst of a sinful world and loved his own even to the end. It is God's own love for the sinner that is seen in God's own self-involvement in the consequences of man's sin to the point of the cross, including the cry of dereliction. That cry – My God, my God, why hast thou forsaken me? – takes place in God, and shows the depths and cost of God's love and forgiveness.

Then, thirdly, we have to say that God's forgiving love does not depend on the death of Christ, but rather is manifested and enacted in it. Alas and alas. All down the history of the Church, Christians have tended to go awry at just this point – the good St Anselm did and most of our good reformers did. But reflect a moment. Is it not grotesque to suppose that God needs a death before he can forgive? I know that the wages of sin are death. Spiritual death is what happens when men cut themselves off from God. That is why men have to be changed as well as forgiven. That is why, incidentally, it is also grotesque to suppose that men are saved by some legal fiction. No, men and women must, in the end, be won over, repent and be transformed by the Spirit of Christ in their hearts and in their midst, if they are to share eternal life. That is why John 3.16 says, Whosoever *believes* shall not perish – and we may add, whether that belief comes soon or late. No, forgiveness does not depend on a death. Rather it is because God loves and forgives that he goes to those lengths to win our repentance and our love. If we insist on asking why Jesus had to die, the only answer is, because men are so wicked. There is nothing on God's side that made it necessary. God incarnate was ready to die because his love, God's love, knows no bounds.

So that is what the doctrine of the atonement is about. It is quite objective. God actually did and does these things. He was there in the life and death and resurrection of Christ. He is here, by Spirit and sacrament, in our hearts and in our midst. The heart of the matter where the doctrine of atonement is concerned was summed up in a nutshell by my favourite theologian, Austin Farrer, and I shall leave you with his words: 'What, then, did God do for his people's redemption? He came amongst them, bringing his kingdom, and he let events take their human course. He set the divine life in human neighbourhood. Men discovered it in struggling with it, and were captured by it in crucifying it.'

I hope and trust that, in the end, we shall all of us, however hard we struggle, be captured by that life and love.

11

THE FUTURE LIFE

My text is Revelation 21, verse 4: 'He will wipe away every tear from their eyes, and death shall be no more, neither shall there be mourning nor crying nor pain any more, for the former things have passed away.'

I should like us to think this evening about the final consummation of God's creative plan in the life of heaven, the new creation beyond death, where there will be no more tears, no more agony and pain, no more death. And I suppose the question is whether we really believe that to be true. It is not only a question that deeply concerns all who want to take Christianity seriously, as we have inherited it from the past. Anyone who suffers the loss of loved ones or

51

indeed who contemplates the world's pain is bound to wonder whether there is a future in God beyond death into which we, our loved ones, and all God's personal creatures will be raised.

1 *The picture language of the Apocalypse*

Our text confronts us with the ultimate Christian hope in the imagery and symbolic language of the Apocalypse or Revelation – very powerful and remarkable imagery – the final battle, the coming of Christ on the clouds of heaven, the millennial rule and then the new heaven and the new earth, new Jerusalem coming down out of heaven from God, prepared as a bride adorned for her husband. Now one thing should be clear to all. We cannot take such imagery, symbolism and picture language literally. That would be simply to misunderstand its character as symbolism. The real question is, what does such symbolism symbolize? Is it really about a transcendental future for creation and for us human beings, beyond death and resurrection?

I firmly believe it is, and will be saying something about that ultimate Christian hope of heaven in a moment. But we need to recall that all down the Christian centuries the Apocalypse's symbolism of a new heaven and a new earth and of a time when God will wipe away every tear from their eye and there will be no more pain or death, has been the powerful inspiration for many groups and movements working for a better world and a better future for men and women here on earth within history, not beyond death. The same is true of that other great biblical symbol, the kingdom of God. Indeed in the Lord's prayer, we pray, thy kingdom come, thy will be done, on earth as it is in heaven. . . And this is quite right, that the picture of God's perfected creation – no more pain, no more tears – should be the inspiration and the stimulus to all to work for the coming kingdom and to make the world a better place, and under God never to rest content with a world containing so much pain, so many tears.

2 *Hope for life beyond death*

But can this be all? In our heart of hearts I think we all know that whatever is achieved here on earth for the removal of the causes of strife, for the healing of pain and for the comforting of men and women in distress, we are not going to see all tears wiped away, all pain removed – not here on earth, not within the historical future, not within the present structures of creation. Most of all is this clear and obvious where death is concerned. For death is not going to disappear in the future of this world as we know it, however improved and transformed it may be. Death is the great problem for all over-optimistic utopian schemes for the transformation of man's condition here on earth. The Marxists, for example, have no way of coping with the ever present fact of death.

So we need, I think, to take seriously the fact that Christianity, like many other religions, has throughout its long history affirmed a transcendent future for creation beyond death. Christianity is in fact one of the chief exponents in the history of religions of the view that man and the universe, as God's good creation, have an eternal destiny, that history has a transcendent goal in the divine intention, that in the end God's creative purpose will be finally realized and that all men and women, past, present and future, will be raised to take part in the final consummation. And that is what the imagery and symbolism of Revelation chapter 21 is all about.

Well, do we really believe that to be true? I think we might and we can and we do, if we take God seriously enough, if we really believe in God as the creator of the world and therefore of the whole world process as something moving under God towards a future goal beyond its present structure, a goal in which God intends us all to share and in which God will be all in all. Of course we need more than just a real conviction of God as creator. We need a real conviction of God's nature as love. We need to know that it is love that made the world, not a stern and faceless legislator. It is when we take God

53

seriously as love that we know death cannot be the end, that the love that loved us into being cannot and will not let us go, that the world of personal being and personal relations, the world of human love and of divine love cannot be extinguished for ever but must be transformed into the imperishable conditions of eternity.

3 *The basis of such hope in the Christian's experience*

But how can we get this real conviction not only of the reality of God the Creator but also of the love of God that will not let us go? Well, I suppose the answer is, we learn this by experience. One starting point is human love itself. Human love so transcends the physical and chemical constituents of our natures as animal organisms that it points to an absolute love at the heart of things. Another starting point is our specifically religious experience, whether mystical or numinous – to use the technical terms for the basic forms of religious experience, the sense of oneness with the infinite source of all there is, and the sense of awe before the ultimate mystery.

But the chief source of our real conviction of the reality and love of God, in face of which we cannot but believe that he will wipe away every tear from our eyes, and death and mourning and crying and pain shall be no more, is the gospel of the incarnation which we celebrate on Christmas day. For love came down at Christmastime. We see that love in the Christ-child and in the astonishing fact that our God is Emmanuel – God with us – not a remote tyrant but vulnerable, self-sacrificial Love.

One of the extraordinary things in the Book of Revelation is the way in which in chapter 21 it is God who says, I am the Alpha and the Omega, the beginning and the end – and in chapter 22 it is Jesus who says, I am the Alpha and the Omega, the beginning and the end. But this identification of God and Jesus, this recognition of God in Jesus, this awareness that Jesus is the human face of God, is precisely what is special about our Christian religion. The Christmas message about God himself, in the person of God the Son, coming amongst us as one of us to make known his great love and to love us back to him, is the key to our knowledge of what God is like and of the fact that it is love that made us, keeps us, and intends us for eternity.

4 *Trust in the God of Christmas and Easter*

Not long ago a friend of mine was telling me how angry she was with God; and God knows, in the tragic and traumatic circumstances of her life, she had reason enough to be angry. But I found myself writing in reply that at Christmastime it is not so easy to be angry with God in a cradle. You see, our anger at God is usually directed at an imagined God, a tyrant, a father figure, a judge, an unmoved mover. But the real God is the God who does not stand aloof, but comes to meet us and to be with us where we are, a God who subjects himself to tears, mourning, pain and death, precisely out of love for us in our grief and pain. By so doing, he wins our love in return and loves us back into loving relationship with himself and with our fellow men. The Christian God is indeed the 'fellow-sufferer who understands'.

But of course to see the bearing of Christmas on our hope of heaven, we have to take Christmas and Easter together. For if the love revealed in the incarnation shows us that God is the sort of God who cannot let us go, the power of God revealed in the resurrection of Jesus Christ from the dead shows us that God can and does overcome death and pain and tears and that he will bring us home at the last.

Whether, then, we really believe that God will raise us and all men from the dead and will make us and all things new, wiping away every tear and abolishing pain and death, depends on how seriously we take the God of Christmas and of Easter, and how seriously we take the incarnation and resurrection of Jesus Christ. For as we sing at Christmastide:

> He came down to earth from heaven
> Who is God and Lord of all
> And his shelter was a stable
> And his cradle was a stall.
> With the poor and mean and lowly
> Lived on earth our Saviour holy.
>
> And our eyes at last shall see him
> Through his own redeeming love
> For that child so dear and gentle
> Is our Lord in heaven above;
> And he leads his children on
> To the place where he is gone.

12

THE REFUTATION OF ATHEISM

There was a time when the social and cultural constraints which affect everyone's beliefs and attitudes certainly favoured belief in God, so that to be an unbeliever was to swim against the tide. Nowadays in much of the western world, though not in Ireland and curiously not so much in America, the social and cultural constraints work the other way and favour unbelief or at least agnosticism, so that to be a believer is now to swim against the tide. These pervasive tendencies are very interesting things. I find it very intriguing to meet so many young people coming up to Cambridge with hardly any Church background at all and hardly any conception of what belief in God might be like. Of course there are

some who have reacted against the religion of their childhood, but far more nowadays have grown up in an entirely
secularized environment and have no clue as to what religion
is about. They view believers at best with tolerance as one
might a member of the flat earth society.

Now whether these social and cultural constraints favour
belief or unbelief has very little bearing on the truth or
falsehood of belief in God, but when it is less fashionable to
believe, one tends to ask oneself more often why it is one
believes, and one tends to be more conscious of the reasons
for belief than when belief can be taken for granted. Since my
own trade is the philosophy of religion, I find myself
considering the reasons for and against belief a great deal of
the time, in lectures and supervisions, as well as in pubs and
in the open air. So I thought I would just give you this
evening some reasons for believing in God, and tell you why,
despite the social and cultural constraints now moving the
other way, I do not think I could ever really succeed in being
an atheist, even if I wanted to.

1 *The cosmological argument*
I shall begin with some pretty well-worn territory – the
classical arguments for the existence of God, which still seem
to me to have some force. Take the cosmological argument.
This is the argument from the world's contingency (I shall
explain that term in a moment) to there being a necessary
ground, cause or explanation of the world's existence. Some
minds get perplexed about the existence of anything at all –
why is there anything and not nothing? – has often been cited
as the most basic metaphysical question. I must say I do not
think that question really gets much purchase-hold. It is too
general. The starting point of the cosmological argument is
not why is there anything at all. It is rather, why does this
complex physical universe, consisting of just such fundamental particles and energies, behaving in accordance with just
such fundamental laws of nature, exist? This is what is

puzzling – the complexity and specificity of the universe that we find ourselves inhabiting. And this is what is meant by contingency.

As far as we can see, there is no inherent reason why the fundamental energies or particles are what they are nor why the fundamental laws of nature are what they are. They might have been otherwise. Indeed some cosmologists speculate, admittedly without much evidence, that they *are* different in other parts of the cosmos. So that is the cosmological argument. A contingent universe like this requires a non-contingent, that is a necessary, ground. Note that the 'why' questions do not automatically carry over to that. If it is contingency that constitutes the puzzle, then a necessary ground cannot be thought of as puzzling in the same way.

I know that a child goes on asking why. Who made the world? God made it. Who made God? But that is because the child is a child and, as the psychologist of education, Piaget, tells us, small children cannot grasp abstract concepts. They are bound to think of God as an old man in the sky or a large-scale father or headmaster or president or whatever. God is bound to appear to the child as no less contingent than the world is, and so the child goes on asking 'why' questions. But we are not children any more. Our minds have learned to cope with abstract concepts and we can grasp the difference between contingency and necessity. We realize that the idea of a necessary ground of the contingent universe's being in being does not give rise to 'why' questions in the same way that the contingent universe does.

That is one argument. I think it has some force. One of the reasons why I would find it hard to be an atheist is that I would be in a constant state of puzzlement at the existence of this complex, contingent, universe. However, I have to admit that to postulate an infinite creative *mind* to account for there being such a universe with such specific properties and laws might seem a somewhat extravagant hypothesis, were it not for the actual nature of what has emerged from the

58

interaction and combination of those fundamental energies in the course of cosmic evolution. This brings us to the design argument.

2 *The design argument*

I think that the fact that the basic stuff of the world has it in it so to combine, and that the fundamental laws of nature make it possible, perhaps inevitable, that from the clouds of interstellar dust an environment productive of life and personal being should have emerged is suggestive of design. This argument has been strengthened by the discovery of the remarkable specificity and narrowness of range of the initial conditions that make it possible for life (and thus rational beings like ourselves) to emerge at a later stage in cosmic evolution. Apparently, unless the total mass of the universe were almost exactly what it is and unless the rate of expansion of the universe after the 'big bang' were almost exactly what it was and is, the possibility would not have existed for the formulation of these elements which were to form the chemical basis of life. The fine structure of the cosmos seems therefore to have had built into it from the start the necessary conditions for the emergence of life and mind. Such a state of affairs suggests intelligent design.

We certainly need at this point some explanation of the nature and extent of suffering and evil in a world supposedly designed. Such an explanation has been given in terms of the general conditions necessary for a world of finite personal creatures endowed with wills of their own and living in a regularly structured environment which makes possible a world of inter-personal life. We cannot go into that now, but, subject to there being some such explanation of the presence of evil and suffering in the world, we now have before us two arguments for the existence of God – the cosmological argument and the design argument – of some plausibility.

3 *Arguments from value*

The third argument is known as the moral argument. Here we turn our attention to the values discernible in human life – the value and significance of human life – indeed the sanctity of life, as it is called – and the values espoused and sometimes realized in human life – the extraordinary goodness of some people and what they do. Even if we are pretty bad at realizing moral values, high moral ideals, merely as ideals, are highly significant phenomena in the world. Admittedly it is disputed whether or not all this is just subjective preference, socially encouraged as the condition of human flourishing. But quite apart from the question whether the conditions of human flourishing do not tell us something about the fundamental nature of things, it is surprising to find how many modern philosophers, on close analysis of the nature and basis of ethics, find themselves unpersuaded by such subjectivist accounts. It seems to me more plausible to argue that the objectivity of moral value is best accounted for in terms of a transcendent source of value beyond the world itself. I would again be reduced to a state of constant puzzlement, if I really had to suppose that saintliness and transparent human goodness are simply the result of certain combination of fundamental particles.

This sort of argument can be expanded in a variety of ways to draw on other features of the phenomenon of man. The sociologist, Peter Berger, has spoken of 'signals of transcendence', features of human life that resist a purely naturalistic explanation – moral goodness, obviously, including the phenomenon of moral outrage at radical evil like Auschwitz or Hiroshima; but he also mentions play and hope, and one can extend the list to include man's perception of aesthetic values, the beauty of the world and the beauty of holiness. There is not time to explore all this, but I will mention one point – it relates to the phenomenon of hope, actually – a point well brought out by Hans Küng in his book, *Does God Exist?* Küng points to the fact that, even in social and cultural environments favouring unbelief, people, for the most part, still manifest in their lives a fundamental trust in reality. They still, for the most part, live confidently and positively, raise families, hope for the future. Such a fundamental trust in reality is hard to justify if reality does not in fact, deep down, justify that trust. Well, that is not much of an argument, so I shall not pursue it here. But is is an interesting phenomenon.

4 The argument from religious experience

So far I have sketched the cosmological argument, the design argument and the moral argument (somewhat expanded to include other values). Now we can come to the argument from religious experience. This has two prongs – first the very pervasive fact that human beings have experienced the world religiously throughout recorded history all over the globe, and secondly, the fact that each of us can discover for ourselves some inner confirmation in our own experience of what all these other arguments (and the argument from revelation which I have yet to come to) seem to be pointing to.

Take the first point first: the fact of religion the world over is a very remarkable fact. It is not just general facts about the world's being and nature, nor even general facts about human values, that lead us theoretically to suppose that there is a transcendent source and intention behind the world's being and value. This alleged transcendent religious object is claimed to have been and to be experienced religiously all over the place by innumerable people throughout history. And the fact of widespread religious experience is another fact about the world that points to the reality of God. Of course there is a problem about the variety of ways in which the transcendent has been experienced religiously, and of course there are alternative explanations of religious experience. Buf if you hold the theoretical arguments and the fact of religious experience together, the alternative explanations

- psychological ones, mostly – do not seem very plausible.

The second prong of the argument from religious experience – our own capacity to experience the world religiously – is most difficult to treat as part of an argument for the existence of God, since it is a private, inner, affair that hardly carries much conviction to someone else unless they too actually have had much the same experience. This is why all religions tend to say, try it and see for yourself. Buddhists are very good at saying this. You have got to tread the 'noble eightfold path' and carry out the techniques of meditation and you will see for yourself the truth of the Buddhist way. Christians say much the same sort of thing. Well, all I shall say in this talk on arguments for the existence of God is that unless you do find out in your own experience that a God-centred view of the world and a God-centred way of life make most sense, then all these arguments will not carry much conviction. On the other hand, the arguments may help to predispose us to take all this stuff seriously.

5 *The argument from revelation*

So much for religious experience. Here now is one more argument – the argument from revelation. Now I mean argument. I am not going to use the appeal to revelation as an argument-stopping device. With all due respect to friends and colleagues, I do not myself wish to say that the Bible is revelatory of God because it says so. I do believe that the Bible and Church teaching reveal God's nature and will to us, but not because they say they do – rather because, on critical investigation, they make most sense of the world and of life. So the argument from revelation goes like this. All the other arguments, the cosmological argument, the design argument, the moral argument (in its somewhat expanded version) and the argument from religious experience should lead us to suppose that there is a transcendent creative mind and will behind the world we live in. If so, we should expect that creative mind or spirit to make itself or himself known by revelation. The religious have indeed made revelation claims. We should investigate them, probe them, test them for their moral, spiritual and intellectual power to make most sense of the world and of life. And all I can say – well, I could say more, but this sermon is getting rather long – is that I have found the Christian gospel of the incarnation and the love of God the creator is a more powerful key to interpreting the significance of life than anything else, however profound, that I have come across in the history of religions.

One final point. The way to *disbelieve* in God is to split all these arguments up and chip away at them separately. The way to *believe* in God is to see – and experience – them all together and to sense their cumulative weight. I am not appealing to revelation and experience apart from my appeal to value, mind and contingency. These matters must be weighed up as a whole. Now I know that sceptical philosophers such as Antony Flew call this the 'ten leaky buckets argument' and say that ten leaky buckets hold no more water than one leaky bucket. But the arguments are not leaky buckets. Each has some force, and together they support the case like the four legs of a chair supporting your posterior.

Well, there you are. I for one do not see how I could be an atheist. Things just would not make sense. What do you think?

13

TRUTH

One of our research students asked me to preach about truth, so I will. And I choose a series of texts, not surprisingly, from St John's Gospel. Before Pilate, Jesus says, 'For this I was born and for this I have come into the world, to bear witness to the truth'. Earlier he had said to his disciples: 'If you continue in my word, you are truly my disciples and you will know the truth and the truth will make you free.' Similarly in the farewell discourses he says of the Comforter, 'When the Spirit of truth comes, he will guide you into all the truth.' And of course most specifically and amazingly of all: 'I am the way and the truth and the life.'

So let us consider: what do we mean by truth? Let us ask the question seriously, not like Pilate with a shrug of the shoulders, What is truth?

Well, our good friend Aristotle remarked that to say of something that it is X when it is *not* X is false, and to say of it that it is X when it is X is true. What could be more simple? Truth is a matter of articulate awareness in thought or speech of how things actually are. Rational beings, and I hope we think of ourselves as rational beings, like to know the truth. We like to know how things actually are. We do not like to be deceived.

1 *Scientific and artistic truth*
Something of this passion for truth is to be found in what makes a great scientific mind. I think I have some sense of what that must be like – very much at second hand – in reading about cosmology and elementary particle physics – the sheer excitement of unlocking some of the deepest secrets of nature and gaining a glimpse of the basic structure of matter and the laws governing its behaviour and interaction over cosmic evolution. No scientific mind could possibly believe that all that is fiction, human construction or invention. It may be a partial, heavily conditioned glimpse into the nature of things, but it really is discovery, a finding, after long and hard search, of something of the real nature of the universe in which we live. There is a deep passion for truth in science.

But we also want to know the truth about man. Of course

science comes in here too, and there are many truths about ourselves which we are now aware of which would have amazed St John and St Paul, and Aristotle too, for that matter. But for much of the truth about man, we turn to literature and great art. For in deep and complex matters like what it is to be human, we need more than a few simple thoughts or statements to disclose the truth about ourselves. Great poems, novels and plays – though in themselves, like scientific theories, human artefacts and constructions – nevertheless can come to disclose and reveal the way things actually are with human life on earth, both individual lives and social life as well.

There was a marvellous talk on the wireless a few months ago by Bernard Levin about Shakespeare. He spoke of the pleasure which seeing a performance of *Love's Labours Lost* for the first time had given him. It was a play he had never seen or read. 'That experience', he said, 'the pleasure of the new-born Shakespeare, sweeping me away on a river of glory, taught me, and teaches me still, whenever I recapture the feelings I had that night, what is the greatest of all the pleasures Shakespeare provides. No other writer has brought us so close to the heart of the ultimate mystery of the universe and man's place in it. No other has felt and presented the numinous with such certainty and power, no other penetrated so deeply into the sources from which he derived his genius and from which we all, including him, derive our humanity. And that is the ultimate pleasure of Shakespeare, the deep, sustaining realization that his work is not only beautiful, thrilling, and funny, but above all, *true*.' That is the point I want to stress. Our eyes are opened by Shakespeare – and others – to whole aspects of human reality of which we had not previously been aware.

2 *Religious truth*
But now, what of religion and especially our Christian faith? Well, here too and, unless something has gone most sadly

and terribly wrong, especially here, we are confronted with what purports to be both revelation and discovery of *truth* – the ultimate and most all-embracing, and yet most personal and particular, truth about God, the universe and man. In Christian faith, the deepest realities of all come to expression in story, ritual, sacrament and word, so that we can come to know the deepest truth and live by it. Anyone who allows himself to be caught up into the world of the Bible and the Christian tradition has embarked on an endless journey of ever deeper encounters with the very basic truth of life. We learn here, in Christian faith, the ultimately personal nature of reality – we learn that this astonishing world whose secrets we unlock in natural science, is the creation of a mind and heart of love. We learn that man, that we ourselves, are not the chance products of blind natural forces, but the children of a Father's love, called out of nature into spirit and destined for eternity. We learn that human frailty and alienation and sin are not the last word, but can and will be overcome; and we learn that the whole world-process, the whole of history and our own lives have a specific purpose, goal and final consummation in the creative intention of the God of love who made us.

These are not easy lessons. The truths of which I am speaking here demand of us commitment, involvement and self-knowledge. It is not easy to admit the truth about ourselves – what we are and what we were meant to be. Christian faith has rightly spoken of judgement, not in a crude sense of justice or desert, nor in a legalistic demand for appropriate distribution of rewards and punishments, but in the sense that the fellowship with others and with God for which we were made simply cannot be achieved without complete self-knowledge and absolute truth. The life of heaven is logically impossible for one caught in the snares of self-deception or inauthentic life. That is why men and women have to face up to what they are and to what they have done, if ever they are to be able to accept forgiveness and be reconciled with one another and with God. This is why the absolutely searching and penetrating love of God can seem a terrible thing to those who have made their lives a lie or who are turned in on themselves and alienated from their own true good. We must not only be forgiven: we must accept forgiveness and allow ourselves to be changed, to grow and to mature into the persons we were meant to be.

3 *Future truth*

All this, you will notice, introduces a subtle twist into our understanding of the nature of truth. At first I spoke of the human mind's passion for truth – our deep desire to know how things really are with the world and with ourselves. But Christian faith speaks of a revelation of the truth, not only about how things ultimately are, but of how they were meant to be and of how they *will* be in the end. A religious perspective opens up an enormously dynamic conception of the world-process in the midst of which we find ourselves. We learn not only who God *is* but also what he will be and will do; indeed we learn not only about the nature of the world, but also about its ultimate future; and we learn not only about the nature of man but also about his destiny. Our topic of truth, then, leads straight into that of the divine *promise*. Our themes so far have been creation and fall – the truth, that is, about how things ultimately *are* with man and the world. Now we turn to God's promise that the love that made us will not let us go but will achieve our reconciliation and enable us to inherit the life eternal for which he made us – in other words the truth about how things ultimately *will* be with man and the world. These future truths, of course, we know, not from science or art, but from God's revelation and God's promises.

4 *Embodied truth*

But now comes the most amazing thing of all, where Christian truth is concerned. For these most profound and most far-reaching truths are conveyed to our knowing minds, not by letter or by an instruction manual along with the world package, but by a particular human life – a life lived and a death died nearly 2,000 years ago, to which the holy Scriptures bear witness. We are not given an ever more far-reaching theory than those of science; nor are we given a work of art surpassing Shakespeare's *Hamlet*. We are given the Word made flesh – a life that *embodies* the truth of God and truth of man – man as he was meant to be. The endless ramifications of his incarnation are, of course, worked out in theories, doctrines such as we pore over in the Divinity School – and in works of art such as Bach's *St Matthew Passion* or Dostoevsky's *Brothers Karamazov*. But the primary embodiment of divine revelation of absolute truth is none of these things, not even the holy Scriptures which bear the most immediate witness to the revelation, but rather the incarnate one himself, whom we encounter not only through the pages of the Gospels but as a risen, living Lord, in prayer and sacrament and in the fellowship of Christians, and also in every human child of God and in the whole creation, whose secret heart and Logos he already is.

At Christmas time we shall be singing and hearing about the greatest of all truths:

> This is the truth sent from above,
> The truth of God, the God of love.
> Therefore don't turn me from your door
> But hearken all both rich and poor.
>
> The first thing which I do relate
> Is that God did man create;
> The next thing which to you I'll tell
> Woman was made with man to dwell.
>
> Thus we were heirs to endless woes
> Till God the Lord did interpose
> And so a promise soon did run
> That he would redeem us by his son.

And at that season of the year
Our blest redeemer did appear
He here did live, and here did preach
And many thousands he did teach.

Thus he in love to us behaved
To show us how we must be saved
And if you want to know the way
Be pleased to hear what he did say.

(English traditional carol)

14

REVELATION

I should like to speak to you this evening about revelation, about God's revelation of himself to us men and women. Some people think that it is wrong to speak of revelation, since if God had really revealed himself to us, revealed his being, his nature and his will, then it should be clear to all. Manifestly it is not clear to all. There are many people who do not believe that God exists, let alone that he has revealed himself to us. Any many others confess only to some dim apprehension of a God who remains hidden and not revealed at all or not very much. Moreover there are quite good reasons for Christians not to claim too much where revelation is concerned. The book of Revelation in the New Testament is about the future, not the present. According to 1 Peter we are 'guarded through faith for a salvation ready to be revealed in the last time'; and according to St Paul we *wait* for the revealing of our Lord Jesus Christ, and we walk now by faith and not by sight.

Even so, we do believe that God has revealed and does reveal himself to us – though for good reasons, which I shall say something about in a moment, he has done so in the past and does so in the present indirectly, somewhat unobtrusively or at any rate not overwhelmingly; and we believe that there is a sense in which God does remain hidden in his revelation – again I say for good reason which I shall come to in a moment. Only in the future do we expect direct, complete and unambiguous revelation.

1 General revelation

Let us think about the less direct ways in which God has revealed and does reveal himself to us. Well, consider Psalm 19: 'The heavens are telling the glory of God.' Some of you will have sung those words to the splendid music of Haydn, who wrote in an age when people did not find it hard to believe that God is revealed in his creation – that the stars and the sun and the moon, the waters of the deep, the mountains, the astonishing world of animals and trees and flowers – that all these things 'their great original proclaim', as an eighteenth century hymn has it . I believe that God the creator is indeed revealed in his works and that modern science, for all its power to explain the interconnections and casual powers of things, has only increased our sense of wonder at the being and the deep rational structure of the universe from the elementary particles up to the galaxies and from inanimate matter right up to man. But of course the creator is not directly revealed. His invisible power can be discerned in his handiwork but he is also hidden behind the given structures of creation, and the problem of evil is a standing objection to any easy reading of the designer from the design.

We are speaking here of what the Christian tradition has called general revelation; as St Paul put it in Romans 1.20: 'ever since the creation of the world God's invisible nature, namely, his eternal power and deity, has been clearly perceived in the things that have been made'.

But general revelation is not exhausted by the disclosures

of the creator's power in the works of creation. It includes too the disclosure of the will of God in the human conscience and the perceived values of goodness, beauty and truth. Again this is not uncontrovertibly obvious. Conscience and the alleged perception of objective value can be accounted for in terms of socialization during our upbringing and conditioning by parents and teachers and social norms and what have you. On the other hand, it has been widely felt, and I think rightly so, that goodness, beauty and truth have a more objective and eternal grounding in the nature of things, and that this too is an indication to us of the divine source of all value (as well as of all being). This too we may think of as part of God's general revelation, this time through the human moral sense.

We may also, I think, speak of man's religious sense the world over, expressed in many religions, low and high, primitive and sublime, as the many-faceted human response to the pressure of God's general revelation by his Spirit to the human spirit. Admittedly the history of religions provides many examples of distortion and abuse by man of his religious sense; but the fact remains that man at all times and all over the globe shows himself to be a religious animal, and that something of God is revealed in human religion as it is in the human moral sense and as it is in the natural world. Of course the religious sense is not a third channel alongside nature and value. To perceive God as the source of all being and value is itself an exercise of the religious sense.

2 *Special revelation*
So much for general revelation. But the Christian tradition speaks not only of general revelation but also and primarily of special revelation – by which it means first and foremost God's special revelation of himself in Jesus Christ. For Christian faith, God has revealed himself most clearly and searchingly by taking our nature upon him and coming amongst us as one of us, demonstrating by costly action his

boundless love, and winning our free and glad response of faith and commitment.

But again, even in special revelation God does not overwhelm us with his glory. He came, as Kierkegaard put it, incognito, born in a shed at the back of a pub, a poor man with nowhere to lay his head, and allowed himself, as Bonhoeffer put it, to be edged out of the world and on to a cross. Nor did Jesus Christ appear on earth by magic out of the blue. His coming was prepared by the long and arduous evocation of a particular religious tradition among the religions of the ancient middle-east, namely the faith of Israel. Even God's special revelation is not blatant and direct. It is channelled through a developing history and tradition and a human life lived from within that tradition, though coming to transcend it by far. Christians believe that that life – the life of Jesus, his teaching, his example, his passion and his death – and that mysterious event, his resurrection – all that is the decisive key and clue to the nature and will of the hidden God.

Note that I have not spoken of scripture as revelation. That is because I believe most firmly that Christ is God's revelation of himself to us, and that scripture is the human witness to the revealing and saving events of Christ's life, death and resurrection. For Muslims, scripture, the Qu'ran, *is* revelation; but for Christians, scripture, the Bible, is the witness to Jesus Christ. He is God's special self-revelation in history.

3 *Present revelation*

But revelation does not come to a head and stop nearly two thousand years ago with the life and death of Jesus Christ. Let me remind you of the remarkable words of Paul in 1 Corinthians 2: 'what no eye has seen, nor ear heard nor the heart of man conceived, what God has prepared for those who love him God has revealed to us through the Spirit'. We saw earlier how God by his Spirit brings home his general revelation to the religious sense of man. Now we see how

72

God's special revelation, the things of Christ, are brought home to us, by the same Holy Spirit of God at work in our hearts and in our spirits as we respond in faith to the love of God in Jesus Christ. In prayer, and worship, and the study of scripture, and especially in the sacrament of Christ's body and blood, the Holy Spirit of God acts in and upon us, revealing God to us – to you and to me – today, and drawing us too into the trinitarian movement of the divine life. We are caught up into God by God's own acts of self-revelation through Christ and in the Spirit.

But you see, none of this has the character of blatant, overwhelming, obvious and incontrovertible revelation. It takes spiritual discernment, faith, to see God in his creation, in human goodness, in the faith of Israel, in the man on the cross, in the breaking of bread, in the conviction of the heart. And we wait for our salvation to be revealed – to be fully, unambiguously and for ever revealed in the end-time, when Christ will reign and God will be all in all.

4 *The indirectness of God's revelation*

So, finally, why this hiddenness, this indirection, this gentle wooing of the spirit through all the created media or vehicles of the divine self-disclosure, which I have mentioned in this address this evening? Well, I do not think it unreasonable for us Christians to assume that God knows what he is doing, that there are sufficient reasons why God sets us in a world whose dependence on God is not an obvious, unambiguous thing. It is not unreasonable to assume that there is a point in God's giving us an ordered, discoverable environment, in his giving us freedom to be ourselves, to grow in the knowledge and love both of creatures and our maker, freedom to seek after God and find him. Above all, when we actually perceive God's way with men and women, his patient wooing of their spirit, his infinitely costly love in coming amongst us in humility and taking on himself the burden of human suffer-ing and alienation – when we actually perceive the utterly personal and loving way in which God comes to meet his creature and win our love in return, this special revelation can, I think, be recognized as something far more precious and valuable – religiously, spiritually valuable – than any obvious, blatant, unambiguous self-revelation of God that men could see without lifting a finger and acknowledge without a thought, like the clouds in the sky.

So let us thank God for his gifts to us, for our creation, preservation, and all the blessings of this life, but above all for his inestimable love in the redemption of the world by our Lord Jesus Christ, for the means of grace and for the hope of glory. Amen.

15

CATCH 22

Some of you may have read the novel, *Catch 22*, by Joseph Heller, about American air force pilots in Italy in World War Two. The catch 22 of the title is this: the doctor can ground a pilot only on two conditions, both of which have to be obtained: first the pilot must be crazy, and second the pilot must ask to be grounded. The catch is that, while a pilot must be crazy to go on flying very dangerous missions, if he asks to be grounded, he can't be crazy, since anyone who wants to get out of combat duty can't really be crazy. The catch is spelled out in the book like this: a certain pilot 'was crazy and could be grounded. All he had to do was ask; and as soon as he did, he would no longer be crazy and would have to fly more missions. He would be crazy to fly more missions and sane if he didn't, but if he was sane he had to fly them. If he flew them he was crazy and didn't have to; but if he didn't have to he was sane and had to.' The hero of the book, when the doctor explained this point to him 'was moved very deeply by the absolute simplicity of this clause of Catch 22 and let out a respectful whistle'. 'That's some catch, that Catch 22', he observed.

1 *The reward motive*

I have often felt that the subject of prayer, spirituality and religious experience has something of a catch 22 quality about it. Take prayer for instance. It cannot be right to urge someone to pray in order to see if prayer works, since anything undertaken in order to see if it works cannot be a prayer; for prayer is the sincere seeking of God's will. Similarly the psalmist urges us to 'taste and see how gracious the Lord is'; but we know we cannot approach religion with that as a motive, since it would be bound to be self-defeating. Anything undertaken just to see how gracious God is cannot be a genuine tasting. For experience of God can only stem from seeking God for his own sake and actually willing the will of God for its own sake – for no other reason than that it claims us with a self-authenticating claim. Outsiders often puzzle over the apparent reward-motif in the Gospels: it looks as if Jesus is preaching love of God and love of neighbour in order to win eternal life, but we know that cannot be right. Such love will in fact yield eternal life, but that is not why we love. Anything done in order to win life will not be love, and it will not succeed in its aim either, for by a kind of catch 22 principle, he who finds his life will lose it, and he who loses his life for Christ's sake will find it, as we read in the Gospels.

Of course it is only a *kind* of catch 22 principle. It is not designed as an inescapable trap which you cannot get out of whatever you do, like the catch in the novel. The spiritual principle that real life can only be found if we forget about ourselves and focus our concern on God and our neighbour does not present us with an impossible goal. The only

75

self-defeating feature of this situation is the fact that concern with self is self-defeating. The catch 22 point here is just that if we turn prayer, grace, eternal life, religious experience and so on into things we want for ourselves, then we will not achieve them; for God's gifts are not like wage packets that we strive for and earn, nor like goods in a religious super-market that we buy for ourselves. This is one reason, incidentally, why Christians are not too happy with transcendental meditation and spiritual exercises undertaken with a view to acquiring spiritual blessedness and peace of mind. For Christ's teaching is that we are not to make our own spiritual lives an object of special cultivation. We grow spiritually when we seek nothing for ourselves, only God's will, as I say, for its sake, and for his sake, and for our neighbour's sake.

2 *Losing oneself*
This basic principle of Christian spirituality, which, if Christians are right, reflects the fundamental truth about our life as human beings – for this is how God has made us – to find our true selves only through selfless actions and concerns – through *really* selfless action and concern, not through some idea of losing ourselves in order to find ourselves – this basic principle conflicts pretty sharply with much modern psychological and educational theory, which puts a great deal of weight on helping people to fulfil themselves, to realize their potential, and aim at self-confidence, self-realization and self-expression.

I remember preaching a sermon at a school in the east of England a year or two ago, and talking about the Christian principle that a man only finds himself through losing himself, as it comes to expression in the great paradoxes of faith in St Paul's writings – 2 Corinthians 6.8-10, for instance: 'impostors, yet true, unknown, yet well known, dying, and behold we live, sorrowful yet rejoicing, having nothing yet possessing all things'. Over sherry with the headmaster afterwards, I was mildly taken to task by him for going on about losing oneself – after all he said, these chaps are just beginning to find their own feet and realize their potential etc., etc. And I suppose it must be rather trying for school-masters who have been slaving away to help young people find themselves to have preachers coming along and saying the best thing to do is for them to lose themselves. There is a clash here and we should be aware of it and ponder it. I do not think we should paper over the cracks and dress Christianity up as an even better recipe for self-realization. For if the catch 22 element is there where I have said it is in religion, then that way of commending Christianity is bound to be self-defeating.

3 *Forgetting oneself*

Actually I am not sure that psychological and educational theories of self-realization are terribly successful anyway, as one might expect on the basis of the catch 22 theory. And I suspect as well that schoolmasters and dons only pay lip service to it some of the time. The real dynamics of human learning in all spheres of life actually emerge when school-teachers and their pupils forget about A levels and success rates and get enthusiastic about something like Shakespeare, when dons and undergraduates forget about things like firsts and the subject itself comes alive, and when, for example, philosophers stop thinking about being professors of philo-sophy and get carried away, losing themselves, as we very properly say, in their subject, as Socrates and Wittgenstein did, to name but two.

I think there are hints here of a recognition even by educationists of that basic principle of the true dynamics of spiritual existence which I have been trying to capture by reference to the catch 22 idea, which put negatively is the principle that concern for self is self-defeating, and put positively is the Gospel principle that a man finds life when he loses it for Christ's sake. For when we turn from education back to religion and ethics, we must suppose, if Christianity has got these matters right, that God has made us for himself (not for our own selves) and that we shall only find our true selves in him. Now, remembering the catch 22 point, we have to say again that that does not mean we turn to God *in order* to find our true selves – that would once again be self-defeating at a higher level. No, we find ourselves by really losing ourselves in God in prayer and contemplation and in response to the claims of God as they bear upon us supremely through the needs of all God's children.

Well, I hope you see the point of what I have tried to say this evening and that this catch 22 element in the spiritual life holds the key to a lot of problems – how to interpret the reward-motif in the sermon on the mount, for example; secular critics who accuse Jesus of preaching a prudential ethic have not begun to see the point of what he says about finding life through losing it. And I hope you see too that while it is perfectly true that we do verify all this in our own experience, as we in fact turn to God and to our neighbour, we do not turn to God *in order* to verify religious belief. We do not and cannot put God to the test like that. Let me end with another quotation from Austin Farrer:

'According to St Matthew's story, Satan suggested to Jesus an arranged experiment on the divine will. Jesus was to jump from the temple cornice and see what the God of the temple would do. But since it was not the divine will that he should jump, his jumping would not be an experiment on the divine will . . .' and then, generalizing the point: 'if we are to experience the sinking of our will in the divine will, then that is what we must be at – the sinking of it, by obedient attention to his; and nowhere else can we have experience of God' (*A Science of God*).

16

OUR EXPERIENCE OF GOD

At some point in commending Christian faith, we cannot avoid an appeal to experience, especially these days, when it is the appeal to experience that counts, whatever we are talking about. This reflects the current crisis over authority in religion as in so many other fields. It is no good just appealing to the Bible or to the teaching of the Church, since the unbeliever will not accept these as having any authority, unless the reality to which they point comes home to him somehow or other in his own experience; and equally what we say will carry no weight at all, unless we too can be seen to be speaking from experience. This means that we have got a double task: we have to make sure that we know what we mean by religious experience and we have to show the possibility of religious experience that can be shared, an experience in which the other can partake and which he can come to find to be as real for himself as it is for us.

1 *Faith and experience*
Even if we say that experience of God is always something given and never something we can get for ourselves – even if we say that God must reveal himself to us before we can know him, this revelation must still speak to our experience, authenticate itself in our experience – or we would never know that an act of revelation had taken place.

But what a difficult task we have set ourselves; for who can honestly say what experience of God is? Many people these days, especially in our western, secularized, technological society, claim not to know what is meant by religious experience, what could possibly count as an experience of God. And our knowledge of psychology – not to mention drugs – reinforces the suspicion that unusual experiences can easily be misdescribed and given unwarrantable significance. Christians too are much less ready than they used to be to talk about experience of God. They are more down to earth. They would rather stick to talking about Jesus Christ as Lord. It seems to be a much more concrete, intelligible thing to talk about the living Christ as Lord of my life and of my destiny than to talk of I know not what experience of God.

But is it really more intelligible? After all when we speak of the risen Christ, we are not just expressing our allegiance to a romantic figure out of the past who is the source of all our inspiration and commitment. To say that Jesus lives is not like saying that Che Guevara lives or whatever. When the Christian says Christ is Lord, he is making a religious claim and it is not so very different from talking about experience of God; for he is making a transcendent claim – the claim that in and through the figure of Christ ultimate reality here and now is disclosed to us and demands our commitment; it is the claim that we really do exist in an infinite context of judgement and grace, and that Christ really is the key to the meaning of our lives – that ultimately we find our true existence and our true freedom in him – not in some past historical figure or in some religious or moral idea, but in one who is a present, living, personal reality now and for ever. To see life like that – for that to mean something in our experience – is, I would want to say, experience of God.

Put it like this. Talk of Jesus Christ as Lord presupposes that talk about God is meaningful, that the world really does point beyond itself to something ultimate, something trans-cendent that can be experienced as gracious, loving, sustain-ing, challenging – something that does give cause for ultimate hope and commitment. So we are driven back, I think, to ask about experience of God.

2 *Mediated experience of God*

What then do we mean, when we talk about experience of God? I do not myself think that we finite human creatures can really claim to experience God directly; even mysticism seems to require some medium through which God makes himself known, such as nature, which for some poets and mystics comes to mediate a sense of the divine, of ultimate, unchanging being permeating all things. I think I can understand that dimly, but I do not know what it means to say that we might experience God directly. Nor do I think that there is some particular peculiar kind of experience that we can pin-point and isolate as being experience of God as opposed to experience of the world or other people or myself. Rather it is these ordinary things – world, people, self – that take on a new dimension of depth, that can come to disclose to us the presence of God and the reality of God, so that we find ourselves wanting to say that we experience God in and through nature, in and through the other, in and through the depths of self-knowledge.

So I think we can begin to collect together those features of our ordinary experience that can come to speak to us of God and mediate something we can only call experience of God. There is, in the first place, wonder – the wonder that comes over us when we come to see the world around us as dependent for its very being and magnificence on a creative will. There is then the whole realm of inter-personal relationship which can come to speak to us of a world of meaning and significance which cannot possible be comprehended in terms of a naturalistic picture of the world as nothing but the interplay of elementary particles. There is the whole realm of value with which we seem inevitably involved and which resists deflation into merely humanistic explanation; but also there is the whole world of religion itself, its heights and depths, its glory and shame, its common perception of man being called out of himself to find his true being in relation to the ultimate source and goal of all there is.

Within this framework, worship and prayer make sense as means of articulating and expressing religious experience. And for us Christians, there is, most important of all, experience of Christ as the revelation of God, reconciling us with God and determining our lives. I have already said that there must be some experience of God, however dim, however fragmentary, before the Christian claim can make sense; but, given that, we must go on to include the specifically Christian experience as among those features of the world which point to God. For to interpret our experience in terms of the Christian gospel and the Christian tradition is itself experience – something actually felt, tested, lived out and found reliable.

3 *Experience and interpretation*
This last point – the reality of Christian experience – brings me to the main thing I want to say to you this evening; and that is that where religion in general and Christianity in particular are concerned, you just cannot separate experience and interpretation. For if I am right in saying that experience of God cannot be isolated and separated from experience of the world, the neighbour and oneself, then there is bound to be a great deal of interpretation involved in the way we experience these things. There is no such thing as bare experience. Inevitably we bring to experience some framework of interpretation, and the experience and the interpretation are inextricably intertwined. For Christians there is a word, a gospel, a living tradition in terms of which a man can experience the world as created, God-given, demanding, yes, but ultimately gracious and accepting. And these things become part of the way we experience the world.

You could put it like this: if the dimension of God is real, if the world is rightly seen as disclosing to us the presence and the call of God in nature, in the other and in oneself, then clearly we cannot separate our experience from the interpretation, the word, the revelation which unveils the mystery in

82

things. Perhaps you will see what I mean if I point to the fact that the Church has always made the sacraments the centre of its life and worship; for the paradigm of our experience of God occurs when we meet at the altar to share the bread and the wine – ordinary things which become the vehicle of God's disclosure of himself to us and gift of himself to us.

In the last resort the test of whether it is all true is whether we actually find meaningfulness, blessing, acceptance and the resources for a purposeful and coherent life, in and through such Christian experience of the world as mediating experience of God.

You see, the unbeliever is liable to demand an external test, as though God were one object among others in the world, which you pick out and identify like a tree or a star. But God is not like that and our experience of God is bound to be different from our experience of any particular thing in the world. The reality of God, I want to say, is disclosed to our experience as we who have glimpsed something of the mystery of things come to participate in the Christian tradition and let the word of the gospel reveal to us the hidden depths where nature points to its transcendent creator, where in my neighbour I find Christ, and where in the depths of my own soul, I find myself confronted by the infinite demand and the infinite mercy of God.

17

THE PROBLEM OF EVIL AND SUFFERING

I want to say something about the problem of evil and suffering in God's world. We all know that God's world contains great possibilities for good – for love, friendship, beauty, discovery and knowledge, for creativity of every kind, for play and laughter – and so one could go on spelling out the positive goods of our life together here on earth. But we know too that God's world contains much evil and suffering – we know this from our own experience and that of our relatives and friends, and every day from the newspapers and the television – terrible accidents, disease, earthquakes, and of course man's inhumanity to man, cruelty and injustice, murder and war.

These things are a great problem for the Christian. They are a problem for the understanding – why does God allow so much evil and suffering in his world? And they are a great practical problem too – what can be done to cope with the world's ills, with one's own suffering and that of others? Is there some way by which evil and suffering may be overcome? Especially we will want to ask whether religion, and particularly, whether Christianity has resources with the help of which men and women can hope to confront the world's ills and overcome them. There's a strange paradox here. I imagine that we all know some people who have renounced Christianity because they cannot reconcile belief in a good, all-powerful God with the facts of evil in the world, and I imagine that we all know people who have embraced Christianity precisely because they have found in it alone the resources and the hope for drawing good out of evil and for the eventual overcoming of evil.

Well, I must try to say something about both problems – the problem why so much evil in the world – and the problem of what can be done about it and what can be hoped for in the end. And surely if we can, to some extent at least, understand why God permits so much evil and suffering in the world, then we shall be the readier to embrace the resources of Christianity for coping with it and overcoming it.

1 *Explaining evil and suffering*
One thing I should say first: it is not easy (or necessarily right) to try to reflect calmly and carefully why it might be that evil

is permitted in the world, when we ourselves or those whom we love are actually caught up in some terrible agonizing situation of destruction, pain or death. I would not try to say the things I'm going to say now if I were visiting an accident ward or if I were a military chaplain on the battlefield. But in a calmer hour when mercifully we are free from the ravages of war, accident or disease, we can perhaps reflect more philosophically about the nature of God's world, and maybe our reflections now can help to sustain our faith and courage if in the future we are called upon to bear the brunt of suffering.

Well, what can we say? It seems to the Christian mind that this world in which we find ourselves is part of a vast creative process in which we and all God's rational creatures are being fashioned patiently and gradually for eternity. In order to become persons we are given a regularly ordered physical universe to be our environment, a universe out of which we have been drawn by the providence of God, working in and through the energies and structures of this physical world. Now we must suppose that there are good reasons why God fashions us this way. We must suppose that some such world as this, operating according to regular general laws which we can come to discover and to rely on, and containing astonishingly powerful energies at every level of its being – we must suppose that some such physical environment and context as this is necessary to our emergence and growth as finite, creaturely persons. Similarly and perhaps more readily we can see that to be persons, we must be free, free both to make or to mar our world.

As we think about the world that God has made, we come to see, then, that the same conditions that make possible a world of free persons, a reliable environment, that is, and real genuine freedom, also make possible the pains and disasters and cruelties that mar the world. I think we have to come to terms with this basic fact of the created universe, that it is the very same general laws and fundamental energies that make possible all the goods of creation and yet at the same time all

85

the possibilities of evil. You cannot, at this early stage in the fashioning of a world of personal creatures, have the beauty of creation without the possibility of ugliness; you cannot have the sensitivities and delights of love and happiness without the possibilities of pain, and you cannot have the freedom to embrace with joy the creative will of God without the freedom to rebel and pursue the paths of hatred and wrong.

But, you may say, if we believe, as Christians do, in resurrection to a life where there is no death, no pain, no tears any more, why must this whole painful process be gone through first before God takes his fragile creatures and translates them into the flawless conditions of eternity? To that question I would hazard a twofold reply. In the first place, it seems, we need some such world as this, relatively speaking at a distance from the God who made us, in which to be rooted and to grow as relatively independent personal beings. Only when we are thus established in being, with God, as it were, hiding himself behind the screen of the universe, so as not to overwhelm us, but to allow us to grow and to find him – not obviously and immediately but gradually – find him for ourselves, that is – only then is the creature there to be immortalized, to be given the gift of a share in Christ's resurrection.

2 *Coping with evil and suffering*

Well, let's suppose that we can see some sense in all this – that we can see partly at least why God makes us indirectly, makes us make ourselves, in and through a universe that is at once the condition of joy and of pain. If we can accept this, certain further consequences can be drawn. We realize that there are virtues and values which depend on the world being a hard as well as a wonderful place. Only because there is evil and suffering in the world can there be such things as courage and co-operation against the odds, sympathy, forgiveness, and reconciliation. Do not get me wrong. I am not saying that suffering is put into the world to make it a kind of moral obstacle race by which we are to learn the sterner virtues. No. Rather, given the fact of evil and suffering, for the reasons I was suggesting just now, then we find that there are ways in which some at least of the sufferings of men and women can be turned to good – that good can be brought out of evil, at least sometimes – and that a creative use of suffering is not beyond the bounds of possibility.

We are turning now to my second main problem. How are suffering and evil to be coped with and overcome? Before I try, in brief, to say just a word about that, let me say in passing that I have in mind throughout this address chiefly the problem of innocent suffering. I do not deny that sometimes by our folly and our wickedness we bring suffering upon ourselves, and that to that extent such suffering is deserved. But the religious mind cannot for one moment rest content with the idea that all suffering is deserved. Already Job in the Old Testament cried out against that idea, and Jesus, in the New Testament, explicitly rejected it, when asked about the folk on whom the tower of Siloam fell. No, I have tried rather to show a more basic reason, in the necessities of creation, not for each particular evil, but for there being the risk and possibility of suffering and evil in these preliminary stages of God's creative process.

So what can we do about it? The key to a Christian practical response to the world's ills is and, of course, can only be God's own way with evil and suffering in the life and death and resurrection of Jesus Christ. In him we see at once the power of the Spirit, making for wholeness in men's lives, and also, when the wickedness of men prevailed, we see him treading the way of the cross, bearing the brunt of suffering and evil in his own person and making it the channel of our redemption – our reconciliation with God. I believe that if we can truly see the cross of Christ as God's cross in our world, if we can see there God himself taking responsibility for the inevitable consequences of creation, making himself vulnera-

ble to evil and suffering and bearing the brunt of it himself,
then we have indeed a morally credible God to trust and rely
on through bad times as well as good. We are disciples of the
one who did not hold aloof, but who came to us and comes to
us to share our pain.

3 *Resurrection*

But there's more to be said. We know too that the cross was
not the last word. Christ rose from the dead, and it is by the
power of the resurrection that he is a living resource of
spiritual strength for us today. Whatever the world may
bring, we know that the love of God in Christ is stronger.
Christian faith is faith in a God who is with us in the depths of
affliction and it is faith in a God who raises the dead.

In our worship and our prayer and in the Holy Communion we draw on these resources; for the risen Christ gives
himself to us here and now in the bread and wine which
signify his body and blood, broken and poured out in a cruel
death. But the sting of that death was drawn. And the sting
of all the world's suffering is drawn too when men and
women allow themselves to become Christ's fellow cross-
bearers in the world, and in their own lives come to manifest
the sure and certain hope of resurrection.

In the end of the day Christian faith stands or falls with the
resurrection. Only in the faith of Christ crucified and risen
and in the power of the resurrection can we confront the
world's suffering and evil with real hope. Paul summed the
whole matter up in Romans 8: 'For we know that the whole
creation has been groaning in travail together, until now; and
not only the creation, but we ourselves, who have the first
fruits of the Spirit, groan inwardly as we wait for adoption as
sons, the redemption of our bodies. For in this hope we were
saved.'

18

HAPPINESS

At the beginning of the academic year in Queens' College we
have a matriculation dinner to celebrate the arrival of the
new students. (We used to call them 'freshmen' but now that
we have gone mixed we have to call them something else; we
can hardly say 'freshpersons', so we resort rather lamely to
'first years'.) On the occasion of this dinner, the President of
the College makes some suitable remarks of welcome to the
'first years', and it always used to amuse me when our
previous President, a distinguished international lawyer,
after welcoming them to the college, used to give them this
advice: 'Be happy'. It is a great shame, he used to say, if you
come to Cambridge with all its opportunities in work, in
leisure and in friendship, if you do not enjoy these next three
years. So, be happy. A difficult injunction, I used to think,
for anyone just to carry out.

1 *The meaning of happiness*
For what is happiness? And how can we set about being
happy? The Greek philosopher, Aristotle, made some very
telling remarks about happiness. He said that, while it is an
end in itself – we do not seek happiness as a means to
something else – nevertheless we cannot just aim at happiness
as such. It is a by-product of doing something, being
something, getting something or giving something. And the
trouble is, there is such a bewildering variety of these
'somethings' that are supposed to make men happy. It is not
surprising that the utilitarians, who hold the single principle
of what promotes the greatest happiness of the greatest
number as determining what is good and right should get so
hopelessly tied up over what happiness is and how you weigh

89

up different kinds of happiness. After all, it was one of the greatest utilitarians, John Stuart Mill, who said that it was better to be Socrates dissatisfied than a fool satisfied. And I am sure that our former President was thinking of higher forms of happiness than that of getting blind drunk and singing rugby songs beneath his window.

The variety of happiness is a well-worn theme. The most extraordinary things make some folk happy – the glimpse of a rare bird, the sight of a new railway engine, the sound of Wagner – one could go on at length. You may know that Snoopy book, *Happiness is a Warm Puppy*, with its marvellous examples: 'Happiness is three in a sandpit and no fighting'. But no doubt our former President was thinking of higher forms of happiness, things like finding a consuming interest in one's work or cultivating interests and causes that will last for a lifetime. I remember he spoke of making lifelong friends in one's time at college. And, of course, he was quite right. These are great and lasting forms of human happiness. Other things which we set ourselves to do or to be are more ambiguous perhaps. I dare say you would be happy if you got a first class degree or a blue or attained later on the so-called glittering prizes. But we all know how such things can so easily turn to dust and ashes in the attainment. We speak of being happy as kings, but King Henry V, in Shakespeare's play, says:

> O God! methinks it were a happy life
> To be no better than a homely swain.

That too is a well-worn theme.

Nor is it at all clear how we can actually *set about* being happy, even in the higher presidential senses of happiness. It often seems a matter of temperament or even of luck. We make friends often by chance acquaintance. A deep and lasting love is not something you can decide to find. It is a gift – a matter of pure grace – and the happiness (or indeed the pain) of being in love is not something you can set out to acquire.

So perhaps we can appreciate Richard Whately's words: 'Happiness is no laughing matter'.

Another point of Aristotle's was that happiness was a lifelong thing. It could not be a matter of flitting like a butterfly from flower to flower. Aristotle defined happiness as activity of the soul in accordance with virtue. For you need the virtues in order to carry out long-term goals; and no man is truly happy who has not learned to pursue worthwhile, long-term, goals over a lifetime.

2 Man's true happiness

Now, where is all this getting us? We are homing in on the problem of what makes for true happiness, of where our deepest happiness as human beings can be thought to lie. This is, of course, a topic on which religion has had much to say. Just to stick to the Judaeo-Christian tradition, consider this from the Book of Proverbs:

Happy is the man who finds wisdom,
and the man who gets understanding;
for the gain from it is better than silver
and its profit better than gold;
[wisdom] is a tree of life to those who lay
  hold of her;
those who hold her fast are called happy.

But now consider the Beatitudes in Luke 6. Blessed (or happy) are the poor, the hungry, those who mourn, the persecuted. Very paradoxical indeed! Of course Matthew's list is not quite so paradoxical. There, in addition, the meek, those who hunger and thirst after righteousness, the merciful, the peacemakers, the pure in heart, are called blessed or happy too.

These more or less paradoxical insights into human

91

happiness only begin to make sense when we take the measure of the religious conviction that God is the ultimate object and source of human happiness. The wisdom of which Proverbs speaks is that which comes from the knowledge and fear of the Lord. The Beatitudes speak of those who have set their hearts on God's kingdom, no matter what the world may do to them. So maybe there is not such a contrast between Proverbs and Luke after all. The Beatitudes just bring out more sharply the fact that worldly *un*happiness is no barrier to true happiness. Herein indeed lies the strength, I think, of a religious perception of man's true happiness. In Augustine's words, God has made us for himself and our hearts are restless till we find our rest in him. You see, Christianity reckons with the restlessness and ambiguity and precariousness and chancy quality of the human quest for happiness – even for the higher forms of happiness of which our former President used to speak. A Christian man or woman knows that in this world you cannot just set yourself to be happy – the world is not made like that – and true and lasting happiness involves a love and a grace and a spiritual power that come from above and carry us through pain, disappointment and *un*happiness, and inspire us to find our true selves in giving ourselves away.

Christianity speaks of eternal life – a new God-centred life 'in Christ' – that yields true and lasting happiness in so far as we are taken out of ourselves into the love of God and of our neighbour. I have been writing a book about heaven and it has been fascinating to see how the Christian mind down the centuries has pictured that final ultimate state of the blessed in God for which we and the whole world were made. The two great images of heaven in Christian tradition are on the one hand the vision of God and on the other the communion of saints. For Christianity, one might say, contemplation and fellowship are the deepest and most lasting, because eternal, sources of human happiness.

3 *The hope of heaven*

But there is a catch, even in this religious perception of where true happiness lies. The happiness of heaven for which we were made should be the source and inspiration and validation of all happinesses, even our earthly happiness here and now. It may indeed sustain us in pain and unhappiness if that is our lot. But it should also be the inspiration of our happiness in wonder, love, fellowship and service, through all our days. One of the saddest things about religion is that the hope of heaven can have the opposite effect of making a religious person turn his back on the world and neglect the things that make for happiness here on earth, both for himself and, worse still, for others. It is terribly sad to see a religious person for whom the hope of heaven has had the effect of making him neglect his work, his friends, the beauty of the earth and, worst of all, the needs of other people.

No, the path to heaven lies through the earth. There was nothing wrong in the former President's injunction to cultivate the higher happinesses of work, friendship and service, and there is nothing wrong with the happiness of fun and laughter too. It is just that it is often rather difficult, and we need the hope of heaven and the resources of God to sustain us through bad times as well as good. But the good earth is the Lord's creation. It is his will that we should find happiness in our work, in our friendships, in our loves, in art and music, and in trying to make the world a better place for all God's children. (Here is one more quotation, from Herbert Spencer: 'No one can be perfectly happy till all are happy.' That is as religious a sentiment as ever an atheist spoke.) But my point is that all these goods are not to be rejected in favour of the highest good. Rather perception of the highest good enables us to see them in their true God-given light, to value them despite their precariousness, and not to be thrown by disappointment in work, love, friendship, art or even service (for we soon discover that we cannot change the world overnight).

So let me end with a text since I did not begin with one. It is Matthew 6.33: 'Seek first the kingdom of God, and all these things shall be yours as well.' I regard that as a gloss on our former president's injunction to be happy.

19

CONVERSION

Conversion is one of those religious words, which tend immediately to set up all sorts of resistances in people's minds. The reason for this is obvious: to talk about conversion is to talk about change, not so much external change but internal change, and while a lot of people are quite happy to press for change in everything outside themselves, very few of us are any good at contemplating or accepting change within. Even the most radical of activists turn out to be extraordinarily conservative where the inner man – one's personality, style, outlook, perspective on life, one's way of relating to people, and so on – are concerned. Most people adopt a defensive attitude to their own personality, even when they are attacking everything else. This is understandable, of course, if one feels that one is oneself under attack. We do not like being got at, we do not like not being accepted for what we are. So, up go the defences, down comes the portcullis, and we peer suspiciously from behind our inner battlements at the man who talks about conversion.

Now that kind of situation – an apparent threat and an automatic defence reaction – is not the kind of situation in which either understanding or communication can take place. So let us suspend judgement, let us not prejudge the issue, let us see if what religious people call conversion is really such a threat, such an intrusion on the personality as sometimes it is thought and felt to be.

1 *An expanded awareness*

I intend to approach the topic indirectly, asking you to think first about the difference between noticing things and failing to notice things. It is extraordinary how one can fail to notice things. It is a commonplace that townspeople in the country-side just do not notice what there is to be seen. Sometimes it is a question of knowledge and experience. One cannot *recognize* something if one has never seen it before. But sometimes it is just a question of alertness and attention. You do not have to know what something is called in order to admire it. But you cannot even admire it if you fail to notice it. The man who walks straight past a great crested grebe without noticing it there, skulking in the pond, surely gets less out of his country walk than the man who sees the bird.

This ability to notice things bears a faint resemblance to religious awareness; for both involve the perception of what might easily be overlooked.

There is another point of comparison. If I point out to you the great crested grebe, with great enthusiasm for its beauty. I am surely not to be accused of aggression. I simply want to share this delight.

Sometimes it is not so much a matter of knowledge nor of attention, but rather a failure to see the pattern, to grasp the form of what is being pointed out. Near Lee Abbey in Devon, there is a finger-post pointing to 'the white lady'; but only on my third visit did I see what was meant, namely, that from that viewpoint the *gap* between two rocks against the sky has exactly the form of a lady in old-fashioned dress. For a long time people look where the finger points, but have no idea what is being pointed out. Then suddenly they *see* it. They see the patch of sky between the rocks *as* a white lady. And they are amazed that they could not see it before. I leave you to apply this analogy.

95

This is all very well, you may say, but these examples only give an extremely slight analogy to what conversion is all about. They hardly involve the person as a whole. That is probably so, although I dare say that person is happier who notices things than the person who walks about with his eyes fixed on the ground a yard or two in front of his feet.

2 *Aesthetic awareness*

But let us consider another kind of perception, namely the aesthetic sensibility required in order to appreciate the works of Shakespeare or Jane Austen. You are all familiar with the deplorable results of trying to force schoolchildren to read these books. They simply do not possess the experience or sensibility to understand the amazing, subtle and inspiring qualities of writings such as these. They react very violently against them, and – sadly – often never return in later life when they are in a position to experience the unbelievably moving and life-enhancing nature of these works of art. Now in this case the acquisition of the necessary sensibility takes time. It is absurd to try to thrust Shakespeare down their throats. Rather we must wait, and in the meantime patiently train and encourage their growing sensibility. It is a gradual process, but nevertheless a remarkable change takes place when eventually one comes to experience for oneself the power of works like those of Shakespeare.

So much for noticing things, grasping the pattern in things. So much for aesthetic perception and sensibility.

3 *Falling in love*

Next, I should like you to consider the different horizons within which people live and think and experience the world. A horizon is a limit – and for each of us our response to life and to the world is bounded by different limits or horizons. Each of us processes the data given us by life in different ways according to the horizons within which we think and feel. Now our horizons can change. This is not now just a matter of noticing particular things we had failed to notice before; but rather our whole horizon can be enlarged, can shift, can come to embrace new dimensions of experience.

One of the most remarkable examples of this is falling in love. Not only is the particular relationship transfigured, but also the whole world is seen in a different light. The poets of love describe how the whole world sings, just as, within the horizon of despair, the world of nature, too, becomes alien and unlovely. Now falling in love is often sudden, but can be gradual too. A long-standing friendship can blossom into love, as we say. But the change is just as great. No longer does one cherish one's independence or hard-headedness: aspects of one's former outlook which one used to cling to resolutely simply vanish away.

Religious conversion is more like falling in love than any other of the analogies I have drawn – though God knows it is only too easy to oversentimentalize religious feeling.

Of course, there are all sorts of conversions, not just religious. One can, for example, be converted to Wagner. What one previously found unbelievably tedious now appears monumental and inspiring. You may not think that is a very relevant example. I agree.

More seriously, some kinds of conversion, far from being a liberating and life-enhancing thing, involve a narrowing of horizons and the imposition of blinkers on one's eyes. Some forms of ideological conversion are like that. A man notices some real feature of society, say, to which he had previously been blind, and then becomes blind to everything else. Notice how different that is from the experience of falling in love – or at least how different it can be. For if love makes us shut our eyes to everything else, something has gone wrong. True love, as I say, enhances the perception and transfigures the whole world. Where horizons are enlarged, the things we previously saw are not put out of view, though they may well be seen in a different perspective.

So, finally, let me speak of religious conversion. Whether it is gradual or sudden, it constitutes a change involving our whole personality. It is like having our eyes opened, our horizon quite transformed, our whole being caught up in a love that knows no bounds. It includes a changed response to the world around us, though not just the world around us; it includes a changed response to other people, though not just other people. Fundamentally, religious conversion is a response, whether gradual or sudden, to God's patient, persistent, wooing of us. The gospel story describes that wooing. And the man who has fallen for that love will describe his experience as liberating, life-enhancing, mind-expanding, if you like. If there was felt to be a threat, experience proves that to have been an illusion; if there were resistances to change, they fall away, like one's cherished independence when one falls in love.

Now I want you to make this discovery. It is not that I want to foist my vision of God on you, still less my theology. I have no wish to take over your personality. All I want to do is to point out that there is a discovery to be made, that there is a divine horizon for us all which the gospel opens up, and which I pray you will find in your own way, as I hope I have found and shall go on finding in mine.

20

FAITH

At the beginning of the new academic year – and for many of you at the beginning of your time as students in Cambridge – it seems a good idea to pause for a few minutes and reflect on the subject of faith. Our lesson from Hebrews 11 suggests this as a theme, and it is a particularly appropriate one, I think, because one's time at university can be – is almost bound to be – a testing time for a man or woman of faith. The increased freedom of life at university, the pressure on us both from intellectual and moral criticism of our Christian faith and from alternative philosophies of life and different life-styles here, and the very process of growing and maturing intellectually and as persons – all this makes it incumbent upon us to consider where we stand as men and women of faith, and to ask ourselves whether we are ready both to persevere and to grow in faith, and whether we are ready to give an answer to anyone who calls us to account for the hope that is in us, as we are urged to do in 1 Peter 3.15, although I would remind you that people who quote that verse usually stop there and fail to go on to the next clause. Here it is in full: 'Always be prepared to make a defence to any one who calls you to account for the hope that is in you, yet do it with gentleness and reverence.' I hope you will remember that bit too – gentleness and reverence towards the other, however, arrogant or insensitive or perverse he or she may seem.

1 *Faith and hope*

I need not apologize for linking that verse from 1 Peter which speaks of giving an account of the *hope* that is in us with my chosen theme of *faith*, since Hebrews 11 itself begins with the well known verse: 'Now faith is the assurance of things hoped for, the conviction of things not seen.' Our faith in the unseen God issues in hope for the future of man and of creation.

Christians have fundamentally an optimistic attitude to life despite their realism about suffering and persecution – all the things the heroes of faith listed in Hebrews 11 endured – just because of their conviction of the reality of God, their faith that this is God's world and that God has an eternal destiny in store for his creatures whom he loves. Let me quote that redoubtable Christian, Calvin (whom we do not entirely approve of on other counts) on the relation between faith and hope: 'Where there is a living faith in the Word of God, it cannot be otherwise than that faith should have hope as its inseparable companion, or rather that it should beget and create it. If we have no hope, we can be sure that we have no faith. Those who believe, those who apprehend the truth of God with the certainty which corresponds to it, which is demanded by it, expect that God will fulfil the promises which he has spoken in truth.' Then he goes on: 'Waiting quietly for the Lord, hope restrains faith, preventing it from rushing forward in too great a hurry.'

Do we agree with that bit, I wonder? In a sense, yes, in a sense, no. It is worth pondering. But to continue with Calvin: 'Hope confirms faith, so that it does not waver in its trust in God's promises or begin to doubt. It revives it so that it does not grow weary. It keeps it fixed on its final goal so that it does not give up half-way or when it is in captivity. It continually renews and re-establishes it, thus seeing to it that it continually rises up in more vital forms and perseveres to the end.'

So our theme of persevering and growing in faith cannot be divorced from real hope in the promises of God and in the eternal destiny of God's creation.

My first point, then, is the close link between faith and hope. Our trust in God is strongly buttressed by confidence and hope in the future of man as God's good creation, whatever the world may do.

2 *Trust in the unseen*

But let us consider the nature of faith a little more closely. Clearly the great heroes of faith listed in Hebrews 11 trusted in God despite appearances. Faith is trust in the unseen God and in a future that is not at all apparent when we look solely at the visible world in all its present disarray. But this trust in the unseen is not an irrational affair. If one thing is clear from what the letter to the Hebrews has to tell us about faith, it is that faith is not blind trust or a leap in the dark; and really the chief thing I want to say to you tonight is that faith as trust must be based in clear conviction, and that our Christian conviction in the reality and truthworthiness of God can and must be defended. We can and must give an answer, an account of the faith and the hope that is in us. Faith is not just a non-materialistic attitude, a spiritual stance that authenticates itself, irrespective of any object, as my friend, the Dean of Emmanuel, has persuaded himself somehow is the case. On the contrary, faith as trust presupposes a firmly based conviction in the reality of God, the truth of the Gospel and the promise of eternity.

This theme keeps cropping up in Hebrews 11: verse 3, for example: 'By faith we *understand* that the world was created by the word of God, so that what is seen was made out of things which do not appear.' Or verse 6: 'Whoever would draw near to God must believe that he exists and that he rewards those who seek him' – not that we draw near to him *because* he rewards those who seek him. Our eternal destiny in God is simply the context in which we perceive the love of God and we draw near to him in love for his love – not just for a reward. But that is by the by. My main point is to stress the clarity with which Hebrews insists on the reality of God, on the object of our faith and hope. And, however important trust is, we cannot trust God to exist. We must believe in the reality of God if we are to trust him.

Now you may well say to me that the heroes of faith listed in Hebrews 11 and their Christian successors at least in New Testament times did not spend much time establishing the facts that elicited their trust through thick and thin (mostly thin) – despite 1 Peter 3.15 and its call to be ready to give an answer. They simply lived by faith and went on trusting in the sure and certain hope of God's promise. Well that is partly true. They did spend a lot of time describing what God had done and demonstrating the depth and the scope of God's love; in that sense they did have to give an account of the hope that was in them. But, despite Hebrews 11.6, they did not have to spend much time demonstrating the reality of God. They lived in times when belief in God in some sense was a universal presupposition. The real problem was what God was like and what God had done. In our time, however, we cannot avoid the question of the existence of God, and I can only express my conviction that in our day, Christian men and women must be ready to give an account, both to themselves and to their friends and contemporaries, of their belief, not just their trust, in God. We must be ready to say why we believe in God, and by that I mean we believe that God exists. As I say, we cannot just trust God to exist. We trust him because we find him to be both real and eminently trustworthy – and that finding, that discovery, must be communicable to others.

3 *Readiness to give an account*
Now the relation between reason and experience in the justification of Christian belief in God, the actual arguments I would use and the actual and possible experience I would appeal to, these I cannot possibly embark on right now at this stage in this address. All I can do here and now is to urge you and invite you not to fight shy of the debates that go on here in Cambridge on the foundations of faith, but to take part in them, to take the risks involved in subjecting your own faith to careful scrutiny, for the sake of sharing it with others. This may mean periods of doubt and uncertainty; but I believe that a Christian faith that has acquired the confidence to take a critical stock of itself and to give an answer to those who call us to account is a much more mature and strong faith than a faith that only survives by erecting barricades against the wicked world and living in an inner circle of pious practice and talk.

The heroes of faith in Hebrews 11 may not have had quite the same kind of tests and trials that we do, but they certainly had to engage with the real world around them and hold firm to their trust in God against attack of a very literal and physical kind. The attacks that come our way may not be so physical. I dare say we will not have to stop the mouths of lions or be thrown into a burning fiery furnace; but we shall face here in Cambridge attacks of other kinds and we must be ready to face them, with gentleness and reverence. They are our equivalents here of the image which Nebuchadnezzar set up and there are other forms here of horn, pipe, lyre, trigon, harp, bagpipe and every kind of music to call us to fall down and worship and tempt us away from our allegiance to the true and living God. May God keep us faithful and enable us both to grow and persevere in faith and to become perceptive and convincing defenders of the faith.

21

SINCERITY AND HONESTY IN RELIGION

What is one to think, when one comes across a passage like
this in Andre Gide's *The Counterfeiters*: 'The deeper the soul
plunges into religious devotion, the more it loses all sense of
reality, all need, all love for reality. . . . The dazzling light of
their faith blinds them to the surrounding world and to their
own selves. As for me, who cares nothing so much as to see
the world and myself clearly, I am amazed at the coils of
falsehood in which devout persons take delight.'

These reflections are offered by one of the characters, after
he has observed a scene in a schoolroom. An elderly pious
schoolmaster says, in the course of some rambling discourse:
'. . . these flowers will keep me company. They have their
own way of talking and tell the glory of God better than men.'
The narrator goes on: 'The worthy man has no conception
how much he bores his pupils with remarks of this kind; he is
so sincere in making them, that one hasn't the heart to be
ironical. Simple souls like his are certainly the ones I find it
most difficult to understand. If one is a little less simple
oneself, one is forced into a kind of pretence; not very honest,
but what is one to do? It is impossible either to argue or to say
what one thinks; one can only acquiesce. If one's opinions are
the least bit different from his, he forces one to be hypocriti-
cal. When I first used to frequent the family, the way in which
his grandchildren lied to him, made me indignant. I soon
found myself obliged to follow suit.'

He describes a great scene between the schoolmaster and
one of his pupils; it ends with an effusive and pathetic appeal:
'Henceforth we will be perfectly frank and open with one
another. . . . There will be no more concealments, we won't
keep anything back in the future, will we? Everything is to be

above board. We shall be able to look each other straight in the face. That's a bargain isn't it?' After which, the narrator goes on, they sank deeper than ever into their box – he of blindness – and the children of deceit.

1 *Religion*

I was reminded of these passages in Gide's book when reading some of the remarks made about religion by school-children interviewed by Royston Lambert in his book about boarding schools, *The Hothouse Society*. There can be no doubt that the way religion is often taught, especially where chapel is compulsory, can be extraordinarily destructive of personal sincerity between individuals. There is the obvious point made by Dr Lambert that 'many pupils resent the dogmatic, narrow and above all compulsory aspect of reli-gion in an institution which, in so many other respects, sets out to inculcate criticism, discrimination, breadth of view, self-direction and freedom of choice.' But there is also a more personal contradiction. Religion is taught in such a way that, far from illuminating existence, far from genuinely interpret-ing reality, and far from fostering real openness and accep-tance and love in personal relations, it leads so easily to insincerity and self-deception.

This is particularly the case in relations between the old and the young, teachers and pupils, parents and children, where it is certainly not restricted to the subject of religion; but it can also be the case more generally between believers and unbelievers, or even between believers themselves. The parson – and not just the parson but often the lay Christian – introduces, often unconsciously, a kind of unfair moral and psychological pressure into what he says, so that the response is almost bound to be insincere. This is so frequently the case that, with the best will in the world one finds oneself, in the parish, say, evoking that kind of inauthentic response. People say what they think the vicar wants to hear. And sometimes they come to believe it themselves, to that self-deception is added to the failure in genuine communication.

I hope I have said enough to show that there is a real problem here – a major problem for ourselves personally as individuals, and a major problem where the communication of Christian faith is concerned. Surely it is a terrible thing that a man with the sensitivity of Gide can say what he says about the effects of religious devotion. Of course, you can simply deny that it is true. I hope very much that your own experience is different. But there is a lot of evidence on Gide's side. You cannot ignore the impression actually given by religious education on so many young minds. And one has only to listen to much conversation on religious matters. Speaking personally I know how often I have been caught and still do get caught in such insincerity and I notice it here in some Christian groups.

2 *Friendship*
By contrast with this, one cannot read the comments of the boys and girls in Lambert's book without being struck by the central role of friendship in their lives. It is clear that in unsympathetic surroundings where one has to be on the defensive so much of the time, real friendship is an oasis in the desert. With one's friends one can relax and joke, say absolutely anything, discuss anything. There is mutual acceptance and tolerance. No longer does one have to be on one's guard, or say what one is expected to say instead of what one really thinks. There is openness and honesty – no guile – in fact the very opposite of the kind of relationship described so vividly by Gide.

Do you not think this contrast between religion and friendship strange? Does religion really involve disingenuousness and self-deception compared with the honesty and openness of friendship? How can this be? After all, you remember that in the Book of Genesis we read that the Lord used to speak to Moses face to face, as a man speaks to his friend.

Another point made by Gide is that the devout seem to him to have lost touch with reality. And if we apply this remark to personal relations, it is surely true that, to the extent to which a relation does involve deceit and self-deception, it is unreal, and conversely, where there are mutual acceptance and friendship between people, there the relationship is real. In company with friends one is one's real self; no longer need one hide behind a mask. Now I suggested earlier that one might expect religion to illuminate reality; hence one's sense of shock when it is suggested that the very opposite is the case.

3 Sincerity

This then is my theme tonight: the kind of personal sincerity and openness and honesty which, as Christian men and women, we ought to have in our relations with each other. I want to suggest to you that all forms of Christian faith and understanding which foster such relationships are right, and that those which impede them in any way are wrong. For, deep down, our Christian faith should teach us that such personal being, such integrity and openness lie at the heart of things, that ultimate reality is like that – that God is like that – and our life together should mirror that deepest reality of all.

The great Jewish philsopher, Martin Buber, has taught us in his famous book, *I and Thou*, that reality is most deeply understood in terms of personal relation. A man who treats everything, including people as 'it' is simply shut off from what is most truly real. Only when the other meets me as 'thou' face to face, am I most closely in touch with reality.

4 Realism in religion

It is easy to accept all this without perceiving its implications. The Christian commitment to truth and honesty in personal relations involves accepting the other as he really is. An appeal to ultimate reality must not be allowed to shut us off from ordinary reality, from the complexity of the world

107

around us, from understanding of and sympathy for what people really think and feel and want and hope for. Our commitment to honest and open personal relations involves, for example, a true perception on the part of the teacher of what is going on in the mind of his pupil. It means not being afraid of what is really going on, not glossing over the evil and anger and aggression in oneself and in the other; it means going on loving in spite of these things. It means great restraint, great tolerance, great forbearance in our dealings with each other. It means identifying with the other, rejoicing with them that do rejoice and weeping with them that weep, as St Paul puts it. And here I think of the writings of Harry Williams, especially his little book of sermons called *The True Wilderness* (Constable). He shows how easily we Christians can deceive ourselves, how costly it is really to accept each other, bear each other's burdens, trust each other with our real selves, our real thoughts, our real desires. In reading Williams, one becomes aware of how insidious is self-deception, how easily we hide from each other, building up barriers between ourselves, turning on the moral and the psychological pressure of which I spoke earlier on. One realizes that Gide is not exaggerating. Authentic Christian love is both costly and rare.

I said just now that the personal relation, I and thou, mirrors the deepest reality of all. For we believe that in God himself there is a similar relation, I and thou; we find a pattern for our lives in the love of the Father for the Son, and of the Son for the Father within the blessed Trinity. And we believe that God loves us with just this same openness and receptivity. We see it in the gospel: openness and receptivity. Jesus knows what is in the heart of man, and he takes their burdens on himself. And he accepts men for what they are; he does not overpower them with his own perfection. In the end he lets them do with him what they will.

Let me mention one more book. It is John Oman's *Grace and Personality* (GUP). Oman was a Presbyterian and

Principal of Westminster College here in Cambridge. His book has helped me as much as any other to understand the gospel. For he shows quite clearly that our relationship to God, and God's relationship to us, just like our relationships with one another, must be most deeply personal. We simply misunderstand the Bible when we interpret its teachings about God's dealings with us as anything less than a gracious personal relationship.

That is why I have felt free to talk about personal relations at the human level and at the same time to speak about God and his relation to us. For, deep down, the same things need to be said, as Paul well understood in his great hymn to love in I Corinthians 13. He speaks there at one and the same time of the love of God and of the love we should have for one another.

Do you remember what he says: Love is patient and kind. It does not insist on its own way. Love bears all things. It does not rejoice in what is wrong. It rejoices in what is right, but it bears all things. And it never ends.

22

PRAYER

Why do we pray? In some ways it is easy to answer that
question. How else can we communicate with God? That is
what prayer is – conscious explicit communication between
creatures and creator, man and God. If as Augustine said,
'God has made us for himself and our hearts are restless till
we find our rest in him', then it is the most natural thing in the
world for us to pray. Man is a praying animal. This is his
destiny – to find God and rest in him. Growth in prayer is
growth into this destiny. When we are open to God, when we
learn to live and move within the dimension of God, when we
respond to God's revelation of himself in Jesus Christ, when
we look for the mind of Christ in all the decisions and
attitudes and policies of life, then there is nothing more
obvious and natural than prayer.

1 *The naturalness of prayer*
This is what strikes me about the words of Jesus about prayer
– their natural quality. Do not make a song and dance about
it, he says, pray secretly. Do not heap up empty phrases –
your Father in heaven knows what you really need, so speak
simply and straight-forwardly: our Father who art in heaven,
hallowed be thy name. . . and so on. Ask and it will be given
to you, seek and you shall find, knock and it will be opened to
you. No problems. Why cannot we just trust the Lord and get
on with it? We should not expect to understand how prayer
works or how God answers it – that is his business. If we do
get a fit of doubts, why not simply pray them away: Lord I
believe, help thou mine unbelief? After, all, we are supposed
to be the friends of God.

   Maybe you do not know what to say – well it is like that

when you do not know someone very well. – it is hard to keep the conversation going – but later, when you know him well it is different; the friendship goes on growing and it is easy and natural to talk together and to be silent together, for that matter. Similarly the friend of God will find it the natural and obvious thing to do to talk to God about what is on his mind. When he is happy he will want God to share his happiness; he will want God to laugh and cry with him, when it is a laughing or a crying matter. When he is perplexed he will ask God what he ought to do. When he is in the wrong, he will look for the forgiveness and the self-awareness he knows God can give. When he is desperate, he will just cry to God for help.

Then there is another thing: he will discover that God has much to say to him – not by some magic supernatural voice from the clouds, but in and through the circumstances of life. Every situation is part of God's language. Your words to me, the gladness in your heart or the sorrow in your eye are God's words to me. When you are on holiday and stand on top of a mountain and watch the sunrise over the sea or whatever – listen, because God is saying to you, this is my world, rejoice with me. When you see a man in need and you are on the point of turning away, saying, it is not my business, there is nothing I can do – listen, because God is saying to you, please do not leave me in the lurch, I thought you were my friend. And do not forget that there are the special words of God, the ones in capital letters as it were: the Gospel, the Bread and the Wine. It is absurd to ask, what use is prayer? You might as well say to your friend, what is the use of talking together, of our admiring this view together, of our sitting in the cafe, chatting about this and that or discussing honestly and openly what on earth one ought to do.

2 *The highest level of evolution*
This explicit, growing relationship with God is the high point of evolution. Now at last over millions of years, the created universe has reached the level of self-awareness, of conscious-

ness that we are God's children. Prayer, you might say, is riding the crest of the evolutionary wave. And this goes to show that it cannot be an individual thing – just me and God; it should involve everyone. The whole human race might now be co-operating with God's providence; indeed the Church exists precisely as the spearhead of such an enterprise. The more people open their minds and wills to the Spirit of God, the wider the concerns that are brought within the compass of our prayers and through them our actions, then the more nearly we are at one with providence, swimming with the stream of God's purpose, helping God to shape up his creation towards its ultimate goal, the consummation of all things, when God will be all in all. Maybe the old man protests, the old Adam, of the earth earthy, and makes us look back or even go backwards a bit – or a lot, for that matter; well then it is a struggle for a while, like Jacob wrestling with God all night until the sun rose; but then we are back on course again – though maybe limping a bit like Jacob. That is why we pray. 'God has made us for himself, and our hearts are restless till we find our rest in him.' As we go on praying we discover God more and more, as we seek we find. And equally if God is real to us, we will pray.

3 *Prayer in a scientific world*

So what is the problem? Well, the fact is that many people do not pray any more. Many Christians may join in with the prayers of the Church at worship, but that is about all. Many of the old methods of prayer have gone dead; there is a malaise in the Church were prayer is concerned. At least, people are honest about this these days. If prayer does not mean much to them, they do not kid themselves that it does. I should like us to resist the temptation of saying, well, that just goes to show they are not real Christians. That is no way to help people with a difficulty. There is no virtue in failing to see the problem. And there is a problem; moreover it is a problem for Christians. It is a problem primarily because,

112

whether we like it or not, things have changed.

We live in the twentieth century, not in the first or the sixteenth. We cannot shut our eyes to the fact that there is an apparent clash between a modern scientific understanding of how the world works, and the old understanding of how God works in the world. I suggested in my account of why pray (a) that we should not worry our heads too much about how God works, since that is his business, and (b) that, if we cannot help asking this question, then we ought to think of him working in and through the natural events of the world and of life, in and through our free response, in and through our actual praying. In fact there was nothing in my account of prayer that need necessarily clash with what we know these days about the world.

But old ideas die hard, especially old ideas of representing God's action in terms of direct intervention. That I believe is what people find so hard to believe. But, you see, this is just what we need not force ourselves to believe. We do not have to decide in advance, on the basis of some ancient cosmology, that we know how God works; we must not dictate to God how he ought to answer our prayers, and then expect experience to follow suit. I believe that if we simply go on praying and look for an answer within our ordinary experience, we shall learn something new about God and his manner of working in the world. We shall learn something about the hiddenness of God, that his strength is made known in weakness, that the resources of the divine power and the divine grace are mediated to us in and through the world around us and the people around us, in and through our own hearts and minds and consciences as we open ourselves to him. And we realize that there must be this hiddenness, this indirection, if God is really to be God and not some extra causal factor in the world, and if the world is to be the real world and not simply appearance.

So I suggest that we think of prayer not so much as a substitute for action, but rather as a new dimension in which a man can live. To pray about a situation is actively to seek for the right answer to that situation in the light of God's will for us, and those for whom we pray. Prayer is the seeking of the mind of Christ; it is being receptive to God's will and God's spirit in our responsible decisions and in our whole approach to life. In this sense I believe we ask and receive, seek and find. So I should be very unwilling to think of prayer as something we resort to when we have exhausted human resources. The Christian man is a man who is open to the divine resources all along – and this means that we believe that God acts through man's reason and will, his commitment, his perseverance, his trust, his readiness to dare, his faith – God makes these things the media of his working in the world.

Similarly the events and situations of life can become the vehicles of God's presence to us and God's act in us – provided, of course, we remain open to him. Of course, there is always the possibility that we slip back into purely human attitudes, that we lose the vision of events and situations as mediating God's word and God's act; our perception becomes clouded, opaque and literally mundane. In other words we stop praying. Only prayer keeps the dimension of God open. Of course God does not stop working just because I stop praying. But I know absolutely nothing of his acts, unless I am in a state of conscious receptivity to him, unless this dimension is open to me, that is, unless I pray. So I can only repeat, as we go on praying, we discover God more and more – as we seek we find. And the more God is real to us, then the more we will pray.

114

23

WORSHIP

One of the things I do is lecture on the sociology of religion. This rather dry subject is occasionally enlivened by one's coming across such passages as the following, from a book by Bryan Wilson, called *Contemporary Transformation of Religion* (OUP). He is talking about the fashionable espousal of new religious styles by 'advanced' theologians such as Professor Harvey Cox of Harvard Divinity School. He describes an experimental service organized by Professor Cox in a Boston discotheque in celebration of Easter. He quotes Professor Cox: 'We wanted to surround the colourful Byzantine . . . Mass with partipatory liturgical dance . . . with light-and-music collages, with physical encounter movements – and also somehow to bring those powerful Old Christian symbols of New Life and shared bread more directly into the service of human liberation.'

1 *A 'modern' liturgy*
'Nearly two thousand people participated' – I am now quoting Bryan Wilson's description. 'They painted peace signs, crosses, fishes, and assorted graffiti on each other's faces and bodies. With silver paper crowns they crowned each other. They painted on long strips of paper attached to the walls. Scenes of war and death were then projected, and in turn were interrupted by "free-wheeling liturgical dancers dressed in black and white leotards", who enticed people "into sacred gesture and ritual motion".
 ' "People who had never danced in their lives stretched out arms and flexed legs and torsos. The lithe solemnity of the movements made me think we should get rid of pews for ever . . . In one group a teeny began humming 'Jesus loves me'

115

and soon her whole arm-and-leg enmeshed group began to hum with her".

'Choruses from Bach's "St Matthew Passion" followed. There was jumping, hugging and moaning, and then communion was celebrated by a Roman Catholic priest, an Episcopalian, two ministers of the United Church of Christ, and Mr Cox. People then chanted the Hindu mantra, Om, and fed each other the communion elements. The kiss of peace "was not just a discreet peck on the cheek". Finally, to a record of the Beatles singing, "Here comes the sun", they rushed out to greet the sunrise, chanting.'

Just occasionally, we have had an experimental or informal service in this chapel on a Sunday evening in place of our regular evening service. I am glad to say that it has never been quite like what I have just quoted, and I hope it never will be like that.

2 *Worship and tradition*

I should like us to reflect for a few moments now about the subject of worship and ask ourselves what we think we are doing when we meet, as we are doing now, and as countless Christians are doing all over the world, to take part in divine worship.

I quoted that description of Professor Cox's experimental service, because it sometimes helps to bring out the real nature of an activity if we contrast it with bogus versions. It might help us if we listen to Bryan Wilson's own comments of Prof. Cox's liturgy. Remember these are the comments of a professional sociologist, not a theologian: 'Whatever else such an event indicates, it makes manifest the disenchantment with the received Christian tradition, which is clearly not regarded as enough, and which may be regarded as counter-productive for those seeking salvation through liberation. In such an experimental liturgy, each exotic bauble is divorced from its context, from its cultural significance, is wanted only for its brightness, to deck out a jollification. The

116

strange symbols are not wanted for their quality as solemn communicators of values, but only as titillations for jaded palates that have experienced too much, too quickly, and too lightly. Without any sustained knowledge, without any awareness of what symbols stand for, of what choices have to be made, of what discriminations are imperative to culture and to human life, these modern men demand everything. Modern communications have produced a new liturgical emporium, from which all items may be carelessly and mindlessly brought together, not to represent an appreciation of the accumulated inheritance of past culture, but merely so that a few people may be *high* for an hour or two. Ecstasy is, of course, an element in religious tradition, but it is never one that has the greatest long-run consequence, until momentary ecstasy is transformed into the lifetime of grace.'

Now I very much hope that we shall not get disenchanted with the received Christian tradition, and that if we are disenchanted with it we will rediscover its meaning and value. I hope that our worship here will not be divorced from its context in the whole nineteen-hundred-year-old Christian tradition, and in the world-wide Christian Church of today. I hope our services here will not just be jollifications and titillations for jaded palates, but that we will take steps to ensure that we know what the symbols stand for, that we will learn to discriminate and to appreciate the accumulated inheritance of the Christian centuries. Above all, I hope that if we are taken out of ourselves and enabled to experience something of the ecstasy of worship and contemplation, this will be something which we will allow the good Lord to build up in us into a lifetime of grace.

3 *The creature's conscious and articulate response to God*
For what are we doing here? We are, surely, making our deliberate, conscious response as creatures to our maker, and drawing on the resources he has given us to make us into his instruments for making the world a better place.

117

Let me expand on this a little. To become aware of ourselves as creatures, given the gifts of life and growth, of freedom, and of all the powers of thought and action that we enjoy, given a world of endless possibilities for good, to become aware of these gifts is surely to become aware of the giver, the one from whom these things all come. And as we learn of his gift of himself to us – his coming amongst us, his self-revelation of enduring self-sacrificial love – our response must surely be one of gratitude. And gratitude I take to be the primary impulse and motive for our worship here.

So we come as creatures, out of gratitude, to our maker. But we do not do so as isolated individuals, nor as a bright new idea which someone has only just thought of. We do not come as isolated individuals. We come as a body, with a shared love and a shared commitment. We inherit a common tradition, shared symbols, words and rituals which have meant much and mean much to countless other folk. It is a long tradition, in which we now participate. We today are being grafted on to a widely ramifying vine, with very deep and ancient roots. We certainly hope and pray that God will go on making new wine out of us, but this new wine comes, if it comes at all, from an ancient vineyard and from a long tradition of vintages. You cannot expect to get the same results by scrapping the whole tradition and starting again from scratch or culling an arbitrary selection of fruits from the liturgical emporium of world religion.

4 *The old and the new*

The dangers of a conservative attitude are well known. To revert to the sociology of religion, it is a commonplace how easily religious movements can lose their impetus and become fixated or fossilized. The pressures for reformation and change must not be smothered. But equally, as is quite clear from the example of Professor Cox, if you cut loose from the tradition, all you get is religious froth. We have to keep the right balance. We do so by looking to the God who

118

says, according to the Book of Revelation, 'Behold, I make all things new', but who is nevertheless the God and Father of our Lord Jesus Christ, the same yesterday, today and for ever, to whom that ancient book the Bible bears witness and to whom we are linked, not just by present spiritual encounter, but by nineteen hundred years of Christian tradition.

Our present Christian experience is mediated to us by symbols with a history. The body of which we are members is the communion of saints – Paul, John, Augustine, Anselm, Aquinas, Luther, Erasmus, Francis, Wesley, Newman, Barth, as well as Mother Teresa and all the Christian men and women who have been an inspiration to you and to me in our Christian lives. We inherit the words and buildings and music and art which has expressed the gratitude of past generations of creatures to their maker. Our words and buildings and music and art admittedly cannot just be repetitions of theirs. But there must be continuity with theirs. This year's vintage is a new vintage, but it comes from the same vine. We need those roots. As John Robinson says, the true radical is the man who goes back to the roots. But the way to draw on the roots is not to hack down the tree but to let the life-giving sap run through your veins.

So I hope you will not be disenchanted with the tradition we have inherited, but will find it possible to use it here to join in the worship and draw on the resourses God has given us, and so let him transform us more and more into a life of grace.

24

TESTING THE SPIRITS

One of the things about being at the university is the way one can get caught up by some prodigious and exhilarating enthusiasm, political or non-political, religious or non-religious. For the man or woman caught up in such an enthusiasm, the contrast between their present enthusiastic state and their former apathetic one is quite remarkable. The condition of one's former, average, a-political or non-religious, uncommitted self, looks pitiably blind by comparison.

1 *Enthusiasm*
The enthusiast, therefore, thinks of those who do not share his enthusiasm as simply blind. And did not Jesus himself complain about the people who would not dance when he piped, and who would not mourn when John the Baptist wept and wailed? Ah, yes, but Jesus *was* from God, so we believe, and so was the Baptist in his way. The other John wisely observes in his first letter that we must test the spirits to see whether they are from God.

You see, one of the dangers of enthusiasm – for example, in the religious case, the claim to direct inspiration by the Spirit of God, is that it smothers reason. But as Austin Farrer, the former Warden of Keble College, Oxford, in a marvellous sermon on 'Inspiration by the Spirit', says, there are not fewer reasons for what God ordains than for other things: there are more, far more. There are all the reasons in the world, if we can find them.

There's the rub: '. . . if we can but find them'. We do need our eyes to be opened, our horizons enlarged, our sympathies quickened, our insight deepened, our vision transformed. All these things we need, but the question is *how* are they to be acquired? Is it really by direct inspiration against all reason? I think not.

No, the choice does not lie between apathetic blindness on the one hand, and irrational enthusiasm, itself a form of blindness, on the other. Those are not the only alternatives. Both in politics and religion, our eyes are really opened when the claims people make, the ideas suggested to us, are *tested* and found to make sense, when they are matched against experience and reality and actually found to illuminate them and to enlarge our sensitivity to the world and to other people's real needs.

Thus in religion it is a serious engagement with the Bible, a critical struggle to find out what it has got to say to us, that will really open our eyes to God's will for us. We find the mind of Christ not by opening the Bible at random and sticking a pin in some arbitrary text, not by waiting passively to be told something by God or by someone claiming to speak for God, but by actively using all our faculties, including our reason, in prayer and thought and conversation.

2 *Reason*

To condemn reason and wait for revelation is like believing that we ought to leave things to Providence. Dr Johnson had the answer to that attitude: 'Providence is not counteracted by any means which Providence puts in our power', he wrote to Boswell. And Providence has put reason in our power.

Farrer, in the sermon I mentioned – it is to be found in his collection of sermons, *The End of Man* (SPCK) – has two cautionary tales, one about a relative who was bedridden for forty years just because she refused an operation on the grounds that the Holy Ghost told her not to have it, and the other of a young girl who made a disastrous marriage just because the Christian group she belonged to persuaded her against her better judgement that that marriage was God's will.

The first case is clear enough. The fear of the surgeon's knife expressed itself as a fictitious revelation and so it could not be argued with. The second case involved the suppression of instinct and sound judgement by group pressure, and just because good judgement was suppressed, the girl could not argue with them. But God does not suppress our good judgement. He makes it better judgement, as we explore our faith, and grow in grace through prayer and sacrament, through honest reflection and the meeting of open minds.

So we are to test the spirits to see if they are from God, by exercising all our powers, of head as well as heart.

3 *Inspiration*

I will refer to Farrer once more. He points out that we say in the Nicene ccreed, 'I belive in the Holy Spirit, the giver of life, who spake by the prophets'. The two functions, say Farrer, lifegiving and inspiration, are one. Precisely by becoming alive, alive to what surrounded them, alive to what God was doing in and through the nation's history, the prophets found themselves speaking God's word. This is the sense of aliveness that one looks for in Christian men and women – the perception and, in this sense, the enthusiasm, of people whose reason is more acute, not less, whose hearts are more open, not less, people who really search the deep things of God, rather than allow themselves to be swept off their feet on to some fanatical or ideological bandwagon.

For the political case is very similar to the religious one. There was an unhappy incident in the Senate House once during discussion of Lord Devlin's Report on the state of the university after a period of student unrest. One senior member accused a student of advancing his political views with the same fanatical conviction of being right that some medieval sects had shown in claiming direct inspiration by the Holy Spirit. He got accused of blasphemy in an ugly exchange. But I am bound to say it was a just comparison. For unless we are prepared to *test* the spirits by which

122

political enthusiasm is aroused, we shall end up just as in the religious case, with closed minds and uncritical attitudes making us ride roughshod over other people and spreading darkness rather than light.

One has only to reflect on what men have done to each other in the name of politics and religion to realize that enthusiasm is not necessarily a good thing. Apathy may be blind, but so is that kind of enthusiasm, and often it has more disastrous results. That is why it is so important to *test* the spirits to see whether they are of God. And as Jesus said, a propos of those who failed to recognize God's messengers, whether they came eating and drinking or whether they came fasting: 'God's wisdom is proved right by its results'. So test the spirits and look honestly at their results.

25

WHY MISSION?

Our former senior fellow had in his possession a letter written by Mahatma Gandhi from prison to his, our senior fellow's, brother-in-law, who was a medical missionary in Kashmir. In the letter, Gandhi criticises the missionaries, albeit gently, because, he says, they have a double aim in what they do. Instead of coming out of love for God's children to cure their diseases, they want to preach to them as well. And so they give the impression to always having an ulterior motive behind the admittedly splendid healing work they do.

This is a very telling criticism. And I think it is true to say that it reflects a mood which has grown since Gandhi's day and in fact has penetrated the Church itself to a considerable degree. We are all aware now of the ambiguities of Christian mission, and there is no denying the fact that the theology of mission is in the melting pot.

1 The justification of mission

I think you will agree that that letter of Gandhi's raises several crucial questions about the Church's mission: its justification in the first place, the motivation which Christians have or ought to have, and the way it is actually carried out. And these questions apply to any kind of mission, to the work of the Church in Africa or India and to our mission here in a largely secular environment. It is precisely the sort of question Gandhi raises that has thrown the World Council of Churches into grave perplexities in recent years, and which also demands from us, if we are honest with ourselves, radical examination of our duties, motives and methods, where Christian witness is concerned.

There is a real problem here. On the one hand it is clear that imperialism, condescension, ulterior motives have corrupted the Church's mission in the past. One can see why, in the thinking of the World Council of Churches, the notions of Christian *presence*, of silent *service*, or at least of genuine *dialogue*, have come to replace the old emphasis on evangelization. And yet on the other hand it is only too clear how the essence of the Christian gospel is lost if we cease to commend God's revelation and God's way of salvation and life for man to others.

This dilemma is inescapable. I suggest that tonight we think not so much about the world-wide mission of the Church as about how this tension – the tension between our duty to preach the gospel and our duty to respect, love and serve our neighbours for their own sake – how this tension affects our own situation here, our attitudes and actions vis a vis our fellow students and teachers in this place.

2 Uncoercive witness

Well, first of all we must recognize this tension in ourselves and not turn a blind eye to it. We must, on the one hand, feel the necessity of bearing witness to the truth as we see it enshrined in the Christian revelation. On the other hand we

124

must feel the force of Gandhi's objection and other similar objections: we must recognize the dangers of imperialism, condescension and most tricky of all, this business of ulterior motive, double aim.

We have come to learn, I think, that we cannot be imperialistic about commending Christian faith. Just as the missionaries cannot ignore and despise non-Christian religions but must respect them and enter into dialogue with them in order to learn what apprehension of the divine they may contain, so with our colleagues and our friends we cannot ride roughshod over their views, their perplexities, their doubts, their hopes. Christian faith must surely commend itself not by force but by attraction. And part of its attraction is or ought to be precisely that it fosters the sort of people who love and accept their fellows for their own sake as infinitely valuable. If people feel they are being got at, or cared for only in order to be won over, then like Gandhi, they have every reason to complain. Love from ulterior motives cannot possibly be pure.

How can we solve this impasse? We are to communicate the Christian revelation and yet that very revelation teaches us to love and accept people unconditionally. Well, there is not one answer to this question. All I can offer are some guidelines, some basic principles, which will, I hope, steer us between the Scylla of arrogant dogmatism and moral pressuring and the Charybdis of silence and the abandonment of missionary endeavour.

3 Truth

I'll restrict myself to two themes: truth and love. We are, of course, committed to the truth – the truth about God, Christ, the world, man, his nature and destiny. It is because we believe that the Christian revelation illuminates these things and makes sense of reality at all its levels, objective and subjective, and so is fundamentally true, that we have a vision to share and a way to recommend. But we have to admit the

125

ambiguities of this vision. We cannot ignore the fact that these truths are not publicly, objectively verifiable – to use the philosophers' jargon. In the nature of the case, they are known subjectively through commitment and experience and by actually following the way of Christ. This undeniable ambiguity where Christian truth is concerned rules out dogmatism and arrogant proselytizing. We can only offer this vision to others gently, perhaps indirectly; for in this situation words often fail to connect. With infinite patience, we can only hold out this vision, hoping that it will attract men's allegiance, as the words and above all the character of Jesus drew disciples to him. (Remember how Jesus loved the rich young ruler, yet in the end let him go.)

It is an implication of our living by the truth, that we must be open to the truth; there is an absolute contradiction between Christian commitment and a refusal to face the truths of science and psychology or whatever. Things have gone wrong if our vision of God blinds us to the truth about ourselves or about God's world. So we must be always learning, always open-minded. How often have men like Gandhi had cause to complain that Christians never listen, but assume that they have all the answers and have only to instruct. That is hopeless. You will know the truth, says Jesus, not, you do know the truth, but you will . . . and the truth shall make you free.

This is one guideline: have nothing to do with anything that militates against the truth – the truth at any and every level.

4 Love

Then secondly, love. I have no doubt that it is the sheer attraction of unconditional, unselfish, love – active care for individuals for their own sake, accepting them, valuing them, bearing with them, laughing with them, weeping with them, for their own sake and for no ulterior motive – that is the genuine hallmark of Christianity. And I believe that no one need listen for a moment to anything that anyone may say about God, Christ, man, the world, heaven or hell, unless their vision of life can be seen to evoke and create this unconditional acceptance of people for their own sake, and this absolute love, conditioned by no ulterior motives whatsoever.

That is the second guideline then: have nothing to do with anything that qualifies love, that subordinates it to some ulterior aim.

These are the tests by which we judge the Church in our own day and at any time: does it serve the truth and does it foster love? These are the questions that matter.

So our answer to Gandhi would be this: we do have two aims. We must bear witness to the truth as we see it – though remember we never have the whole truth. And we are bound to love our fellow man absolutely and unconditionally. There *are* two aims. But you see, they are both absolute. We do not subordinate one to the other. The commitment to truth is not an ulterior motive, subordinating or qualifying the claims of love. Equally the claims of truth are not subordinate to those of love – that is sentimentality.

The trouble with Hinduism – and for all his admiration for Jesus Christ, Gandhi remained at heart a Hindu – is that it has a woolly idea of truth. All religions somehow are aspects of the truth and it does not matter which you believe. That is a woolly doctrine; you might as well say it does not matter whether you accept relativity theory of not, since all physical theories have something in their favour. And where love is concerned – well, it is hard to say. We often think that Gandhi was a better Christian than the Christians; but where did he get his absolute commitment to his fellow men from? Perhaps it is significant that in his letter from prison to our senior fellow's brother-in-law he appeals to the example of Jesus, when criticizing the missionaries for their alleged ulterior motives.

Well, be that as it may. The one point I have tried to make

127

this evening is this. We do have two aims; but both are absolute. For God's sake do not let the one become an ulterior motive for the other.

26

OTHER RELIGIONS

My text is from Matthew 8.11: 'I tell you, many will come from east and west and sit at table with Abraham, Isaac and Jacob in the kingdom of heaven . . .'. And it will not surprise you that what I have in mind in choosing this text is the great mystery of the faith of other men – of how we are to regard the great non-Christian religions such as Hinduism and Buddhism. Having just spent seven weeks in India and Sri Lanka, the one country predominantly Hindu, and the other predominantly Buddhist, I have been thinking quite a lot about this problem. Inevitably one's ideas change when one converses with men and women of faith from another culture and religion, and when one converses with Christians, Catholic and Protestant, who constitute pretty small minority groups in a Hindu or a Buddhist environment. In such conversations, one becomes very conscious both of the strengths and weaknesses of one's own religious community, and also of the strengths and weaknesses of those other great religious traditions too.

1 *Exclusivism and pluralism*
I do not find it plausible or realistic or indeed either humanly or christianly possible to write off the faith of other men as of no revelatory or salvific value. It is impossible to disregard the philosophical profundity, the devotional fervour, and the deep spirituality of the Hinduism at its best. (At its worst,

128

like any religion at its worst, it is frightful). And it is impossible to disregard the serenity and compassion of the Buddhists at their best (though again, as in Sri Lanka in recent months, the very worst side of Buddhist communalism have been evident).

On the other hand I do not find it plausible or realistic, or at all religiously meaningful, to say that all religions are really saying the same thing or leading in the same direction. That is usually a casual or superficial judgement, quite ignoring the deep difference of practice and belief that characterize the religions – say, Buddhism, Christianity and Hinduism at their best. I do not myself think it right or possible for Christians to think of Christ as one great prophet or guru among others.

Between these two extremes, I look for an understanding of the significance of Christ for the whole world which does justice at once to his uniqueness and finality and to the depth and power of non-Christian spirituality and faith.

2 *Vatican II approaches*

Intimations of the right approach are to be found in the Declaration on the relationship of the Church to Non-Christian Religions – one of the documents of Vatican II. The developments in Roman Catholicism in our time really are amazing. Here is a Church which used to say quite categorically *extra ecclesia nulla salus* – outside the Church there is no salvation – paying tribute to what is true and holy in all the world's faiths. Let me read you a paragraph or two:

'From ancient times down to the present, there has existed among diverse peoples a certain perception of that hidden power which hovers over the course of things and over the events of human life; at times, indeed, recognition can be found of a supreme Divinity and of a supreme Father too. Such a perception and such a recognition instil the lives of these people with a profound religious sense. . . .

129

Thus in Hinduism men contemplate the divine mystery and express it through an unspent fruitfulness of myths and through searching philosophical inquiry. They seek release from the anguish of our condition through ascetical practices or deep meditation or a loving, trusting flight toward God.

Buddhism in its multiple forms acknowledges the radical insufficiency of this shifting world. It teaches a path by which men, in a devout and confident spirit, can either reach a state of absolute freedom or attain supreme enlightenment by their own efforts or by higher assistance. . . .

The Catholic Church rejects nothing which is true and holy in these religions. She looks with sincere respect upon those ways of conduct and of life, those rules and teachings which, though differing in many particulars from what she holds and sets forth, nevertheless often reflect a ray of that Truth which enlightens all men. . . .'

How is it possible to speak so positively of what is true and holy and good in other faiths and at the same time to speak of Christ, as the text goes on to do, as 'the way, the truth and the life'?

The answer, I think is to speak inclusively rather than exclusively of Christ. If Christ is indeed the truth of God, the Logos at the heart of all things, then it is not unreasonable to see that universal truth or Logos in whatever is true and holy and good in other faiths.

3 *An inclusivist approach*
Really there are three possible ways of thinking about Christianity and other religions – there is exclusivism, there is pluralism and there is inclusivism.

The exclusivist approach is the view that, since Christ and Christ alone is the way, the truth and the life, only those who explicitly accept him as such can experience the revelation, the peace with God, and the eternal life and wholeness that he brings.

The pluralist approach is the view that all the world faiths are channels of approach to God and saving knowledge of God. Christ is indeed the way, the truth and the life for Christians, but Krishna, say, is the way, the truth and the life for Hindus, and the Buddha is the way, the truth and the life for Buddhists. Behind these seemingly different culturally shaped and conditioned faiths, is the same, many-sided, infinite and absolute divine reality, accessible to all, by one or other of these diverse paths.

The inclusivist approach is the view that Christ is indeed the culmination of God's self-revelation of his nature and his will for all mankind. But since it is God's truth, God's way and God's life that are there in incarnate form in him, there is a universality about Christ that enables us to detect his spirit present already, perhaps implicitly, perhaps in a hidden way, in all that is true and holy and good. Christ's truth, just because it is God's truth, includes all truth. Christ's way, just because it is God's way, includes and is reflected in all goodness.

I think this inclusivist approach to be the right one. It makes sense of the Gospel text I used at the beginning – that 'many will come from east and west and sit at table with Abraham and Isaac and Jacob in the kingdom of heaven'. It makes sense of the story later on in the same gospel in which those who feed the hungry, clothe the naked, visit the prisoners and so on are received by Christ as having done it to him.

An inclusivist rather than an exclusivist approach is to be discerned behind the title of a famous book, *The Unknown Christ of Hinduism*. The idea is that, just because of the universality of Christ, the spirit of Christ is already there – albeit unknown – in whatever is Christ-like in the faith of other men. Of course this is not a view that would be accepted

131

by the Hindu or the Buddhist. They are likely to reply by speaking of the unknown Krishna or the unknown Buddha of Christianity – or else perhaps to affirm the pluralist position, and I am not denying that there are still fundamental questions of truth and falsity at stake here. But it is a more plausible Christian view than the hard-line exclusivist view, which just writes off the faith of other men.

4 Consequences of inclusivism

An inclusivist view affects the way Christianity is lived and preached in a non-Christian land. Instead of rejecting everything in the other's culture, tradition and faith, and seeking to bring Christ to him as something totally new, the missionary looks for signs of Christ's presence and action there already in the traditions and faith of other men. He seeks to relate Christian faith and worship and action to the indigenous spirituality and culture. Remarkable experiments are going on in Catholic and Protestant churches in India and Sri Lanka, in Christian ashrams and new forms of Christian liturgy, where all that is true and holy and good in Hindu and Buddhist culture is being used in the expression of explicitly Christian worship. Again, an inclusivist approach requires Christians to work with men and women of other faiths or none, to help the sick and the poor and the oppressed and to make the world a better place for all God's children.

There was a beautiful artistic expression of this inclusivist approach in the chapel of a seminary I visited in Bangalore – a College of that ancient Church allegedly founded by St Thomas in South India in the first century. Each side of the altar there were two large murals, one, on the left, depicting the Spirit as a dove, brooding over and inspiring all the world's religions, represented by their symbols – the crescent, the star of David, the reverse swastica (a symbol of Hinduism) and so on. On the right, the mural depicted the figure of *Christus Consummator* – Christ who fulfils and brings to consummation all the intimations of God and aspirations

132

after God that have been given through the universal presence and activity of the Spirit of God and of Christ throughout the history of religions.

So I commend this inclusivist view of the universal Christ to you, as something more intelligible and more deeply Christian than the older exclusivist view. We should be glad to discover that there are innumerable 'anonymous' Christians in the world.

27

CHRISTIAN ETHICS

Christian ethics is my theme tonight, and because we are talking about God's will for us and for the world, I shall have to divide my remarks into two sections and say something both about Christian personal ethics and about Christian social ethics. For we are concerned not only with the will of God for us as individuals in our immediate relations with our fellow human beings, but also with the kingdom of God, with God's will for the whole world, and that means talking about social ethics too.

1 *The basis of Christian ethics*
Now there can be no doubt that the basic principle of Christian ethics is love. For God is love and God is the source and goal of all that is good for us and for the world. It is God's love that has made us, God's love that has redeemed us, God's love that inspires us and comes to shape our lives if we will only let him work in us and through us in the world. If we would only love with something of God's love, there would be little more that need be said about Christian ethics. St Augustine was quite right when he summed up the heart of Christian ethics in the famous words, 'Love God and then do

what you will'. For, if we really loved God and God's love really dwelt in us, then what we would will would be nothing other than the outworking of that divine love in our lives and in the world.

But of course we are not in fact so close to God for talk of love to be enough. We need to spell out that ultimate idea, that ultimate source and goal of all our good, much more concretely and specifically, in terms of moral principles and norms of action, if love is to have any structure, any shape in our lives and in the world. And of course it is spelled out in the teaching and example of our Lord, in the lives of the saints, in conscience and the moral law, in the accumulated wisdom of mankind and of the Church. It is naive to think that we can just appeal in every situation straight to the ultimate principle of love.

But neither is it a matter of settling moral questions by quoting scripture. That is not the function of scripture – well, sometimes it is, as when the Pope said 'Thou shalt do no murder' on his visit to Ireland. But the real function of scripture, as of prayer and sacrament, is so to put us and keep us in touch with Christ and in a living relation to the Spirit of our God, that we grow in the knowledge and practice of what the love of God means for today's world.

Of course we begin to learn the shape and structure of this love from the story of Jesus, his words and his deeds, and especially his passion and his cross. In Jesus and his way we see the very love of God in action. From those marvellous parables, from his dealings with people, from the way he made himself vulnerable, from his patience in adversity, we learn something of the qualities of care for individuals, self-control, steadfast commitment to truth and to God's will which must come to shape our lives in our very different world and our very different vocations. Similarly we see St Paul, out of his encounter with the living Christ, beginning to extract the principles of Christian ethics; first the basic principle of love, as in 1 Corinthians 13, then his well known lists of the fruits of the Spirit, and then his application of all this to actual decisions over concrete issues, like what to do about food sacrificed to idols, that arose in his own life and work in a gentle environment.

I pick that example just to show that the problems change and responsible decisions cannot be made in advance. We do not know in advance what the problems will be. *We* do not have to bother about food sacrificed to idols. Our problems are different. So already in Paul's writings the pattern of Christian ethics is beginning to emerge – a living relation to God in Christ, a recognition of the primacy of love, a spelling out of what love means in terms of basic attitudes and principles and norms of action, and responsible decision in the face of problems and circumstances as they arise.

2 *Moral rules and moral problems*
Let me now say something about the place of moral rules in Christian ethics. One things is quite clear. Rule keeping is not the purpose of morality. Rather moral rules serve love; they spell out the framework within which alone people can learn to love. Morality is for persons. If people are to be loved, to be treated as ends in themselves as God's children, each of great value as a person made in the image of God, then there can be no question of murder, stealing, lying, adultery, coveting and so on. Of course those are absolute prohibitions. But the positive purpose of that framework is growth in love of people.

Let me also say a word about a number of current moral issues in order to show you what it means to say that morality is for persons. Just because the Church sets such value upon persons as being the children of God and the objects of his love, it has always taught respect and reverence for human life, condemning suicide, euthanasia and abortion. But the reason why these issues are so controversial even among Christians is that it is not always clear how these prohibitions (unlike the ones mentioned in the ten commandments)

135

actually do serve love; and one is bound to say that the Church has sometimes gone quite wrong over these matters, as in refusing to give suicides Christian burial or in failing to show forgiveness in cases where people have been driven beyond endurance. And on any view one might well suppose that reverence for life is not served by striving officiously to keep alive.

On abortion, while I am horrified by the way some people speak so casually about incipient human life in their campaign for abortion on demand, in ways which degrade their humanity and cheapen human life beyond belief, I could not possibly endorse the rhetoric of those who speak of hundreds of thousands of murders of innocent children every year. For the foetus is not yet a person and indeed before the central nervous system is hooked up we cannot even speak of a rudimentary person. Abortion is a great evil – we must respect potential and incipient human life – but it is not murder, and *sometimes* it may properly be regarded as the lesser of two evils.

Christian sexual ethics has come under quite a lot of attack in recent years and sometimes justifiably; for again the spirit of understanding and forgiveness which should characterize the attitudes of followers of him who said, 'Judge not that ye be not judged', has all too often been conspicuous by its absence. But if morality is for persons then surely it is clear that high standards in sexual ethics are taught by the Church for the sake of fostering love and a high valuation of persons. People must be helped to learn to subordinate sex to love. People are not and must not be allowed to become just objects of desire. That said, I am sure we could be without the censoriousness and legalism in these matters that have plagued the Church so often in the past. It is an encouraging fact that wherever in recent years the Churches have appointed committees of experts to advise on sexual ethics, marriage and divorce, homosexual relationships and so on, their reports have invariably shown great sensitivity to people and to putting people first. It seems that at least when people study these problems, they realize that morality is for persons.

3 *Christian social ethics*

Well, it is time I moved on to Christian social ethics in the wider sense of Christian concern for the right ordering of human affairs in society at large and indeed throughout the world. It has been argued, and I think rightly, that love, universalized, is justice, and that work for justice within one's own society and internationally is an inescapable dimension of Christian action. I think here particularly of two great twentieth century Christian theologians who have realized this and argued powerfully for Christian participation in the struggle for justice – the American, Reinhold Niebuhr, and the Swiss, Karl Barth. Niebuhr showed very clearly how Christians have often got morally confused by sticking simply to the exercise of charity and benevolence while at the same time conniving in an unjust social structure; and Barth, in his last lecture courses in Basel before he retired, was expounding the Lord's Prayer and its clause, Thy Kingdom come, under the heading, *fiat justitia* – let there be justice. (And of course there is plenty in the Old Testament prophets to support that emphasis).

So concern for politics and for social and political change, both nationally and internationally, is an inescapable aspect of Christian ethics. I am quite prepared to admit that it is not always easy to say what justice actually is in a given time and place. It is often easier to detect injustice in the world. I do not say that we should all, as Christians, jump on a particular political bandwagon. Responsible Christian decision and responsible Christian action in these as in other matters require discrimination and prayerful reflection and a critical distancing from many particular programmes and ideologies, especially those which tend to ride roughshod over people.

So, unlike some of my friends, I am not going to launch into an attack on Mrs Thatcher at this point. On the other hand, maybe I should – for Christians ought to care about the consequences of present policies. But let it be enough for now if I say that Christians and the Churches need to do more than just support the charities and the relief agencies – expressions of Christian love in action though those undoubtedly are. Again it is encouraging that the Churches today, through local, national and the World Council of Churches are tackling these issues, usually, if not always, with genuine Christian discrimination. That qualification is necessary, because it it not always apparent in the World Council of Churches' pronouncements, particularly, that the concern it is expressing is the concern of the crucified one – the concern of a love which works not by force but by persuasion, by making itself vulnerable by its readiness to suffer for the beloved.

4 *Christian love*

Well, let me, in conclusion, come back to first principles. Ideally, Christian action in the spheres of both personal and social ethics, is the expression of the divine love working in and through us, whereby both we and the world are gradually conformed to Christ. We are, by our response to God's own love for us in Christ and his Cross, to grow in love of our neighbour and become, more and more, channels of Christ's continuing love for all God's children. We cannot restrict this love to our immediate neighbour. It must embrace all God's children.

Now realism insists that love of all God's children will take a different form from love of the immediate neighbour. We cannot care personally face to face, for all the people in the world. I have suggested that this universal outreach of love takes the form of the quest for justice. But the divine love (agape) on any reckoning is not just a matter of emotion and feeling. It it that – think of Jesus weeping over Jerusalem.

Much more, though, the divine love, to be mirrored in us, is a matter of will and set policy – a disinterested other-directed concern, whether the other be our friend or neighbour here in Cambridge or the victim of oppression and injustice in Campuchea or Chile. Moreover it is a love which is prepared to take the burden of the world's ills upon itself. We must never forget that the triumph of the love of God in us and through us in the world can only be the triumph of Christ crucified.

28

THE AUTHORITY OF THE BIBLE

The authority of the Bible is an important topic for Christians to reflect on – both for their own clear understanding and for their commission to bear witness to the truth of God.

I shall begin with my conclusion, so that we know where we are going. I should like to be able to win your assent to the view that the authority of the Bible is strictly parallel to the authority ascribed to Jesus in Matthew 7.28 and 29, where, at the end of the sermon on the mount, it says: 'And when Jesus finished these sayings, the crowds were astonished at his teaching, for he taught them as one who had authority, and not as their scribes.' Similarly, I shall be urging, the Bible speaks to us with authority when we read it and find in what it says something truly astonishing, that cuts to our heart and fills us with conviction of the truth of God and of what God has done. The authority of the Bible, in other words, consists in the religiously compelling content of its message.

1 *The variety of sacred scriptures*
Well, that is my conclusion. Now for my starting point. Although my own main work lies in the philosophy of

religion, I find myself increasingly having to make forays into the territory of the comparative study of religions and into the question of the aims and methods of inter-faith dialogue. And this makes me aware of the great variety of scriptures in the world religions. It is quite unfair to speak only of Judaism, Christianity and Islam as the 'religions of a book', though clearly for Jews the Hebrew Bible, for Christians the Old and New Testaments, and for Muslims the Qur'an, play a uniquely normative role in their respective faiths. But the Hindus too have the Vedas, the Upanishads and the Bhaga-vadgita, the Sikhs have the Adi-Granth, the Taoists have the Tao-te-ching, and the Buddhists the Pali scriptures. Of course these scriptures are very different: some express the religious insights of ancient sages into man's relation to absolute reality; some set down the teaching of a spiritual master on the way to find enlightenment or salvation; some provide God's law for man; some bear witness to God's acts of revelation.

The Qur'an, for example, is alleged to consist of divine teaching communicated directly by God to his prophet, Mohammed. The Qur'an itself, so Muslims believe, is in a literal and direct sense divine revelation. The Christian Bible, by contrast, is a much more variegated affair; it embraces writings stemming from nearly a thousand years, poems, sagas, histories, legal codes, prophecies, proverbs, letters, gospels, and visionary tracts, by innumerable different writers, some known and some unknown. This variegated collection is held by Christians to speak with authority not because it was dictated by God but because one way or another it points away from itself to God's self-revealing acts, culminating in the teaching, death and resurrection of Jesus Christ and the continuing presence of the divine Spirit in the Church. I shall be saying more about this anon. At the moment I am simply stressing the great difference between the scriptures of the various religions, as becomes clear from comparative study.

140

Another point becomes apparent as we consider the
scriptures of the world religions in the context of dialogue
between representatives of different faiths. We cannot possibly in that context appeal to any one scripture, as if it was an
agreed authority. Only when a man has discovered the truth
of God and been cut to the heart by the words of the Bible
does the Bible come to have authority for him. In conversation with men of other faiths and indeed with unbelievers,
Christians cannot just appeal to the Bible as if it were an
agreed authority. They can only argue and plead the *content*
of the Bible as something worth pondering, something which
they have found religiously compelling, something which
must be *shown* to be convincing and liberating, and of
universal importance for any man.

It is interesting to note that St Thomas Aquinas, in the first
of his great Summas, the *Summa contra Gentiles*, writing a
text-book for the Christian missionaries to use in Muslim
lands and in conversations with the Jews, does not appeal to
scripture as an authority at all. He knows he cannot in that
context. He simply defends the faith with a power of
argument probably unequalled ever since. In his other
Summa, the one written for Christian theological students,
the *Summa Theologiae*, of course he appeals to scripture –
though he spends a lot of time interpreting it and arguing for
his interpretations – because in this context scripture is
authoritative; for Christians it has already been recognized to
speak with authority, as it bears witness to God's self-
revealing acts, culminating in the incarnation and in the
bestowal of the Spirit. But note that even here it has to be
interpreted and explained.

2 *The content of the Bible*
Let us turn, then, to the actual content of the scriptural
witness – the thing that in the end, one way or another, must
convince with its own inner spiritual power and authority. It
is, of course, God's own revelation of himself as Love – a

141

revelation not in word only but in very deed, the deeds of God
to which the Bible bears witness, and especially the great act
of God recounted in the story of Jesus Christ, in whom we see
God himself, in the person of his Son, out of his great love for
mankind, making himself vulnerable to the conditions of
human existence and bearing the brunt of human wickedness
and suffering. We find in the Bible too the record of the first
response to the risen Christ, as in the power of the Spirit the
first Christians come to constitute the continuing Body of
Christ in the world.

So it is these great truths of God – God our creator, God
our redeemer, and God in our midst and in our hearts –
together with the promise of God's kingdom and God's
eternity that give the Bible, which points to these things, its
great authority. For without the witness of prophets and
apostles we would have no access to the deeds of God in
which he made his love and purpose known. The truths I
have mentioned are not general truths deducible by human
reason. God has revealed himself in history, and the immediate witnesses to his revealing acts are essential if their truth
is to be handed down and grasped by us today. Christianity
does not just go on developing and cutting further loose from
its origin. Christian *understanding* of its origins will indeed
go on developing, but it must be controlled by the events of its
foundation – the life, death and resurrection of Jesus Christ.
So, however sublime our theology, it must go back again and
again to the record of its origins.

Karl Barth, the greatest of modern theologians, used to
speak of the three-fold form of the Word of God – first, the
primary revelation, Jesus Christ himself; second, the written
word, the scriptural witness to that primary revelation; and
third, the preached word, the contemporary exposition of
these truths of God as living realities making men new and
whole in and through the Christian Church today.

Now, humanly speaking, a case could be made for thinking that the great saints of the Church and great teachers like

Thomas Aquinas and Karl Barth, were greater men of God than say Haggai or Jude – to choose a couple of not too controversial examples. But the fact remains that the Church could have got on without Aquinas and Barth, but it could not have got on without its primary witnesses, the immediate witnesses to the crucial acts of God, and, as I say, especially to the cross and resurrection of Christ.

3 *Inspiration and infallibility*

So I do not think we have to say that the men who wrote the books of the Old and New Testaments were uniquely inspired, in a way no other men of God have ever been. They were inspired by the Holy Spirit, but so are all who respond to the gospel in faith. What gave the biblical writers their special place in the providence of God was simply that the revealing acts of God took place among them, there and then at that particular time and place in history.

Nor need we suppose their writings to be infallible in every particular. They were all too human witnesses, whom providence has given a unique responsibility simply to bear witness to something that had happened in their midst. There is no reason to suppose that they fully and perfectly grasped what had happened. We have to penetrate through their fallible human witness to the truth of God and of what God did in the events concerning Christ. There and there alone lies the infallible truth which the Bible enshrines.

Well, maybe I exaggerate a bit. I am not denying that men like Paul and John were out of the ordinary run of Christians, in whom the Holy Spirit came to dwell. Those men in particular certainly rose to the unique occasion that called forth their apostolic witness. The Church was certainly right and certainly acting under God when it canonized their writings and not others; for the Church recognized that they spoke with authority. But what made them authoritative was the manner in which they succeeded in bearing telling witness to the truth and acts of God.

Now if it is the content and the message that counts, if that is what confers authority on the book, we need have no fear whatsoever of biblical criticism. Close study of the Bible can only lay bare more clearly and more comprehensively the content of this book and put us in closer touch with the realities to which it points.

4 *The power of the message*

The authority of the Bible, then, consists in the fact that it confronts us with a message about God's love and about God's promises – his love enacted in the cross of Christ, his promises confirmed in the resurrection of Christ and the gift of the Holy Spirit. By the power of that same Spirit the message of the Bible speaks to us with authority, touching our hearts and awakening our faith in God our creator, redeemer and reconciler.

At the beginning of this address I quoted Matthew 7.29 where it says of Jesus that he taught the people with authority and not as their scribes, and I suggested that in a similar way the Bible speaks with authority when what it actually says astonishes us by its spiritual power in bringing home to us the truth of God. There is another passage, this time in John's gospel, that we can perhaps transfer from Jesus to the Bible in a similar way. In John 7 the Pharisees sent officers to arrest Jesus but they returned without him, and the Pharisees asked them, 'Why did you not bring him?' The officers answered, 'No man ever spoke like this man'.

Similarly many people have taken up the Bible to criticize or to mock, and found themselves saying, no book ever spoke like this book speaks. Of course there is no guarantee that people get the message completely right just by picking up the book. It must be interpreted and expounded and explained, within the community of Christians. But, for all that, it is the content of this book that matters. May it be our experience, yours and mine, that the words of the Bible come or continue to win our assent to the incomparable message of God's love that they contain.

29

UNCOMFORTABLE WORDS

This morning's readings from the Bible (Ezekiel 21.25–27 and 22.1–2, 23–31. Luke 13.22–end) are very far from being comfortable words. They express judgement; they call for repentance and renewal, and they prophesy disaster if that renewal does not take place. Moreover, we know that in both cases disaster came. Ezekiel's Jerusalem fell to the Babylonians and the people were carried off into captivity. The Jerusalem so poignantly apostrophized by Jesus was utterly destroyed by the Romans in AD 70.

1 *Prophecy*
We listen to these words, and perhaps we feel uncomfortable parallels with our own time, especially in this country, which seems to many people to be out of control, spiralling downwards towards disaster. It may be difficult to believe this as we sit in this beautiful place, surrounded by an amazing wealth of resources in art and science; but we have only to go home or back to work, or open a newspaper or turn on the television, to experience the nagging fear that something has gone very wrong, and that things could go to pieces here.

But to prophesy, in such a situation, is not an easy task, nor one to be undertaken lightly by the preacher or the sage. We certainly cannot just transfer the words of Ezekiel or of Jesus to our own time, as if there were no differences between Jerusalem in 590 BC or AD 30 and Britain in the world of today. Nor do recent attempts from archbishops downwards to stop the rot inspire much confidence either in their judgement or what is really wrong with us, or in their vision of what our life as individuals and as a society might be.

For if we are to speak of judgement and repentance, we have to get the diagnosis right, and we have to get our vision of the cure – the alternatives to which we hope men will be turned, if they repent – clear and true. In Christian terms, we must discern correctly what it is that is preventing the realization of God's kingdom here in our midst, and we must have a true vision of his will for us men and women, of what, that is, the kingdom of God on earth would actually involve.

2 *Diagnosis*

I shall say a word about each of these: diagnosis and cure. First diagnosis – judgement. There is a tension here which we Christians cannot escape between the need to see and state clearly what is wrong with our society, our attitudes and our lives, and the need to be non-judgemental in our actual dealings with individual people. It is the tension to be seen in Jesus himself, who both denounced the scribes and Pharisees and also said, Judge not that ye be not judged. Maybe our own case is not so problematic, since we ourselves so clearly fall under our own judgement, when we try to say what is wrong with Britain today.

A further difficulty is the sheer complexity of the modern world. Christian comment is liable to seem both ignorant and naive, in face of the complexity of the economic and international pressures which we face. Yet some things still seem luminously clear. Do you not agree that, for the most part, we in this country do not work hard and conscientiously enough, we expect a higher standard of living than we earn, we restrict our interest and concern much too much to our immediately family and friends, we collude too readily in inequalities and class divisions in our society, we allow standards in work, education, public life to drop, we set our sights much too low and fail to pursue the good, the beautiful and the true, and above all, above all, we fret and fuss about our own problems, when for half the world's population the basic needs of life are not being met. It is this lack of real

146

concern about the widening gap between the rich and the poor nations that seems to me to cry out for judgement in Britain and the West today, and is most comparable to the conditions that cried out for judgement in the Jerusalem of Ezekiel's day.

3 *Cure*

Now what would it be to repent? It would be to let ourselves be transformed and opened up to the needs of the whole world. It would be, in the words of a well-known prayer, to refuse to live in contentment while we know that our neighbour has need. That would be the first mark of the kingdom of God in our midst. But genuine repentance, it seems to me, should bring us a widening of horizons in every sphere. We would cease to be content with the second rate, we would refuse to be trapped in class attitudes or social inequalities, we would resist the temptation to think only of our own families and friends, let alone just ourselves, we would exert ourselves to do our best in our work, and live more simply within our means, freeing our time and energy and money for meeting real needs here and abroad. In such ways we would let ourselves become more ready instruments for God to use in building up his kingdom on the earth.

I trust that it is clear to you that the transformations of interest and concern of which I have been spreaking in such terribly general terms, though they involve a change of heart, an inner awakening, cannot be thought of simply in individual terms. Here, more than anywhere, we need to recover the insistence of the Old Testament prophets that God is interested not just in individual souls, but in social and political justice. The themes of judgement and repentance and renewal concern the structure sof our common life, socially, nationally, and now more than ever internationally. As the poet Donne wrote, 'No man is an island', and no Christian can pursue a solitary path to perfection. But, equally, we cannot suppose that social and political attitudes can be

changed without an inner transformation. The judgement
must strike home, the needs must actually be felt by each of
us, and each of us must receive some real vision, even if only a
glimpse of what God's kingdom on earth might be. And that
personal conviction or conversion is the narrow door
through which a man must pass if he is to become a living
channel of the Spirit of God in the world.

Such a thing can happen. It happened to a young British
soldier in Ulster called Nick White, who went back to Ireland
when he left the army to work for peace, and ran a scheme in
Belfast for Protestant and Catholic children to play together.
He was murdered by gunmen for his pains, but his work goes
on there still.

4 *Conversion*

Men can be changed, sometimes dramatically, sometimes
gradually. A man's eyes can be opened to real needs where
before they were blind, and to wider horizons where before
they were blinkered and his vision parochial. Of course one
has to admit that there are conversions which bring a new
kind of blindness with them. Ideological conversions often
take this form. A man's new-found commitment to the
revolution and to a new society in the future can blind him to
the human realities around him, to the plain truth about
himself, and to the evils which he is prepared to perpetrate in
the name of a better future. Even religious conversion is no
guarantee of a wider vision.

Nevertheless the aim and object of all Christian judgement
and repentance, surely, is to allow oneself and to help others
to be set free, free from the narrow confines of a life centred
on oneself or on the immediate circles of one's family or
friends or class, or on the immediate attractions of our
consumer society, or even on one's own country to the
neglect of the world's poor. And Christians believe that it is
God who comes to meet us in the poor of the earth, in the
unlovely as well as the lovely things, both of which can and

148

must inspire us to let go our narrow self-centred, yet ultimately self-destructive worlds. We believe that it is God who opens our eyes and enables us, by his forgiveness and his grace, to repent, to turn again, newly inspired and with a fresh vision. We believe that it is the Spirit of the living God who will turn us all, if we will let him, into instruments with which to make, not just our country, but the world a better place. If only we would listen to his voice.

30

WAR

Many of you will have heard and some perhaps sung in Benjamin Britten's 'War Requiem', composed for the dedication of Coventry Cathedral in 1962. On the first page of this score, the composer quotes the words with which the young poet, Wilfred Owen, who was killed in the trenches in 1918, prefaces his *War Poems*:

> My subject is War, and the Pity of War
> The Poetry is in the Pity.
> All a poet can do is to warn.

1 *Remembrance*

I find it hard to speak on Remembrance Sunday. I can only just remember the last war, and I had no close relative who was killed in it. And for me the First World War is something to read about, with horror and fascination, in the history books and in the memoirs of those who survived. But of course I have spoken with people who remember both wars very well, people in this country and in Germany where I studied for a year – people who lost sons or fathers in the fighting or whose families were wiped out in the bombing. I remember lunching in Kassel in West Germany with a charming lady whose husband had been brutally killed and whose daughter had been raped by Russian soldiers at the end of the war. I have read books about the wars, about the atrocities committed in Nazi Germany, and about the whole-sale slaughter of innocent women and children carried out in the bombing raids by the Germans over London and Coven-try and by our own forces in the massive raids of 1945, such as the one which destroyed Dresden, a beautiful old German city of no military significance, flattened within weeks of the end of the war, at a time when it was full of refugees fleeing from the Russians. And of course I have read about Hiro-shima and Nagasaki and the unbelievable suffering and death dealt out there.

So, even if we were fighting a just and necessary war to preserve our freedom and rid the world of an evil and mad tyrant – as I believe we were – I cannot see what happened as a simple question of good against evil, right against wrong. To read about these things is to be conscious all along the line of the evil and waste and 'the pity of war'. I know that there were countless men and women who showed astonishing bravery and endurance and who gave up their lives for their country in the face of unutterable horror and brutality. Others died unnecessarily through stupidity and cowardice and fear. Without the sacrifice of all these men and women we would not be where we are now. This is not to be forgotten.

But that does not make war a glorious thing. For all the films and books that tell of heroic exploits and brave sacrifice, I believe that the truth about war is rather to be found in a poem like this – it is one of the War Poems of Wilfred Owen set to music in Britten's War Requiem:

What passing bells for these who die as cattle?
Only the monstrous anger of the guns.

Only the stuttering rifles' rapid rattle
Can patter out their hasty orisons.
No mockeries for them from prayers or bells,
  Nor any voice of mourning save the choirs –
The shrill, demented choirs of wailing shells,
  And bugles calling for them from sad shires.

What candles may be held to speed them all?
  Not in the hands of boys, but in their eyes
Shall shine the holy glimmers of goodbyes.
  The pallor of girls' brows shall be their pall,
Their flowers the tenderness of silent minds,
And each slow dusk a drawing-down of blinds.

Each year on Remembrance Sunday we are invited to come together to remember before God those who were caught up in the fighting and the destruction of war and who lost their lives there, some bravely and honourably, achieving much by their sacrifice, others, as I say, unnecessarily, achieving little or nothing, but all of them ordinary people like ourselves, who were called on to bear the brunt of situations that had got out of control, situations that demonstrate the folly and wickedness of man, and the precariousness of the whole human enterprise. Strangely enough, it seemed to me, while I was in Germany, that the Germans have a much clearer idea than we do of what a remembrance service is about. They know that their people who lost their lives in the last war were fighting in the service of an evil and unjust regime, for which they have not only had to dissociate themselves utterly, but for whose atrocities they have had to bear a terrible sense of guilt. But they too lost friends and relatives, fathers and sons, ordinary men and women who were fighting for their country just as ours were. So they meet on their day of remembrance simply to mourn the dead. I believe that is what we should be doing. We mourn for those we knew and loved and for those we have only heard or read about, like those whose names are recorded here on the walls

151

of this chapel. We mourn also for the world which could not prevent the horror and destruction of the two world wars.

2 The problem of evil

Here I must digress for a moment. For it is a great problem for the religious mind, well, certainly for the Christian mind, why God allows so much evil and suffering in the world. It is a problem to which I personally have found myself giving a great deal of attention in the course of my work in the philosophy of religion. For men and women caught up in the terrible suffering of war, this problem of evil is an urgent pressing existential problem that can utterly overwhelm the mind. For us, mercifully at some distance from the immediate realities of war, suffering and death, it is perhaps possible to reflect more calmly on the necessities involved. For surely there must be very good reasons why God our creator allows his creatures unlimited freedom to make or mar their world. We have to suppose that real freedom is a necessary condition of personal being, of our growth and life as persons in relation to each other and to God.

Moreover we have to suppose that a regularly structured world, law-governed and reliable, yet flexible enough to permit the emergence of novelty, rationality, freedom and creativity, is a necessary condition too of creaturely personal being. Now it is these two factors – a law-governed physical universe and unchecked creaturely freedom – that make possible not only all the good and beautiful and creative things of life, but also all the possibilities of suffering and evil in the world, of which war is perhaps the most terrible and pervasive example.

These reflections may not bring us much comfort, but they help us to understand why God permits the world's ills. And of course there are other things to be said, religiously and, more especially, Christianly speaking. For Christians believe that this life is only part of God's overall plan, that we are involved in a creative process that does not end with the

152

deaths of individuals, whether those deaths come late at the end of ripe old age or early on the battlefields of Europe or in the skies over London. For Christian belief, there is the hope of God's future, for a share in Christ's resurrection, and for a consummation of all things, when death and pain and tears will be no more.

3 An incarnate God

Christians also believe that God himself does not remain aloof from his creatures' sufferings. One of the reasons why in these last years I have found myself quarrelling rather fiercely with my fellow theologians about the doctrine of the incarnation is that to preach a purely human Jesus deprives the Christian faith of its most powerful conviction about the way the problem of the world's evil is confronted and overcome by God himself. For Christians believe that, in the person of Christ, God himself, without ceasing to be God, has made himself vulnerable to the world's suffering and evil and borne the brunt of it himself. To my mind, God is a morally credible God only if we can in all seriousness speak of Christ's cross as God's cross in our world. In another part of his War Requiem, Benjamin Britten juxtaposes the Latin text of the Agnus Dei – O Lamb of God that takest away the sins of the world – with another of Wilfred Owen's War Poems:

> One ever hangs where shelled roads part.
>   In this war He too lost a limb,
> But his disciples hide apart,
>   And now the soldiers bear with Him.

4 Reconciliation

To return now from my digression to the theme of remembrance: the last thing we must do now is to try to perpetuate or renew the hatred or the feelings of hostility of the war years. We mourn for what happened in the past, but our task,

153

as Christians, for the present and the future, is the continuing task of reconciliation – a task symbolized by the young Germans who came over to Coventry to help with the rebuilding of the cathedral, and by the young English people who went to help in the rebuilding of Dresden.

I remember going to Coventry in 1962 to hear Benjamin Britten's War Requiem in the cathedral on the occasion of the festivities marking its dedication. Originally Britten intended the solo parts to be sung by a German, a Russian and an Englishman. It is a comment on the continuing madness of the world that the Russian government refused to let the Russian soprano come, though you can hear her voice on the records that were made later. But even so it was an extremely moving experience to hear Dietrich Fischer-Diskau and Peter Pears sing together in this act of reconciliation. In the last poem the two enemies meet beyond the grave:

> I am the enemy you killed, my friend.
> I knew you in this dark; for so you frowned
> Yesterday through me as you jabbed and killed.
> I parried, but my hands were loath and cold.

Then they sing together:

> Let us sleep now. . .

And the choir embraces their song with the Latin words of the Requiem:

> In Paradisum deducant te angeli. . . Requiem aeter-
> nam dona eis, Domine; et lux perpetua luceat eis. . .

May they rest in peace. Amen.

31

PEACE

I take the fact that we have been more than usually confronted on our television screens of late with wars and
rumours of wars, and that we now await the imminent arrival
of cruise missiles here in Cambridgeshire, as an excuse for
devoting this short address to the topic of peace. In two
weeks' time, I might add, we shall be celebrating in our carol
service the message of the angels: 'Glory to God in the
highest, and on earth peace, good will toward men'.

1 *The gospel of peace*
Christians, as disciples of the Prince of Peace, should of
course be men and women of peace. They should know
something of the inner peace which comes from the knowledge and the love of God. Experience of forgiveness and
acceptance, the recognition of meaning and purpose in life,
Christian spirituality, prayer, meditation, participation and
growth in the dimension of the Spirit, all this should yield
inner peace. Christians should be at peace with each other. In
the Eucharist they celebrate Christ's peace with the kiss of
peace, and, as at the end of this service, we will receive
together as a body the peace of God which passes all
understanding.

Christians should be influences for peace, both as individuals and as the Church in the wider world around them. They
should exemplify how to be at peace with themselves, with
each other and with their neighbours. They should be
peace-making, reconciling factors in the community and in
the world. And of course they should work for peace,
together with all men and women of good will, and in
particular they should work for the removal of the causes of

strife. For there can be no true or lasting peace, nor any deep reconciliation, without justice and freedom. I take injustice and tyranny to be a deeper cause of strife than hate and jealousy, pride and impetuousness because these vices feed on injustice and tyranny and cannot be cured while they prevail. Of course it helps to have inner peace even in unjust conditions. But I fear it is unrealistic to think that you will ever get widespread inner peace among the people at large without tackling the injustices and tyrannies which feed hatred and cause strife.

All this means that the peace of God does not mean peace at any price or at any cost. Much as I admire the pure witness of unqualified pacifism in the Quakers, for example, and in many individual Christians in all the Churches, I could not myself accept that unconditional pacifism is right. It is a sobering thought that many of your predecessors here whose names are inscribed on the wall of this chapel might well not have had to die if the weak policy of appeasement had not prevailed in the period between the wars. And one of the things we learn from Alexander Solzhenitsyn is the resoluteness with which tyranny and the lie must be withstood and opposed. And it is a sad fact of human life in this wicked world that a willingness to fight may in fact preserve the peace better than a total renunciation of all force.

2 *Peace movements*

Christian commitment to peace and work for peace should therefore be discriminating. Christians should not only learn to control, or rather subject to God's control, the passions that make for violence and war, but also the passions that carry so many well-intentioned people into support for foolish policies that may well only exacerbate the troubles of our divided and distracted world. I fear that we can see just such a case in the so-called 'peace movements' of our time in face of the intolerable nuclear threat under which we live. The way in which the peace movement has largely become infected and manipulated by the enemies of truth was made clear to me two years ago when I sat in a room in Moscow with a delegation of European teachers of ethics being harangued by the chairman of the Moscow peace committee. I confess that it was not inner spiritual discipline that kept me sane, but the thought that in an hour or two's time I would be in the Bolshoi Theatre watching Eugene Onegin – *Mea culpa, mea culpa*!

A word at this point about the nuclear threat. Like you, I have thought a lot about this terrible thing which looms over our lives, and I have noticed the enervating fatalism which has overtaken so many, especially young people, today. I have read *The Church and the Bomb* (CIO/Hodder) report and the recently published rejoinder, *The Cross and the Bomb* (Mowbray). It seems to me that, while the waging of nuclear war could never possibly be justified, the only sensible road to peace is that of arms limitation, mutual reduction and multilateral disarmament. And I wish that the moral energy and idealism which are going into CND could be devoted to putting pressure on governments to pursue these policies, though, admittedly, there is a strong case for opposing dangerous escalations and wasteful expenditure in the arms race.

I do not think that Christian men and women ought to give way to the pagan mentality of fatalism on this matter. In fact, I do not think nuclear war very likely, and I believe that God has endowed mankind with a greater instinct for self-preservation than to allow it to happen. But if we should not be fatalistic about the bomb dropping, neither should we be fatalistic (or over-optimistic) about it not dropping. Every Christian man and woman and the Christian Churches as organized bodies of opinion should of course contribute to the cause of genuine peace, not only by supporting policies most likely to keep the peace, but also, by working, as I say, for the removal of the causes of war.

3 *Biblical prophecy*

Perhaps I should just add a warning about the curious idea that nuclear war is foretold in the Bible and therefore is bound to happen. Admittedly the relevance of biblical apocalyptic imagery has been widely recognized in this age of the nuclear threat. Armageddon is a powerful symbol. But it is not a matter of prophecy in the sense of prediction of what will happen thousands of years later. That idea of biblical prophecy is sheer superstition and should be resisted by every intelligent Christian – and by unintelligent ones too. Prophecy and apocalyptic are rather a matter of discernment of what is in man and of the possibilities and dangers that exist if man goes his own way in defiance of the gospel of peace and love.

Such awesome possibilities should send us back to God and to dedicate ourselves afresh to be God's messengers of peace – and that, as I have said, is a matter of letting God work in us the grace of inner peace, letting him build us up into the fellowship of Christians at peace with one another, and letting him inspire and enable us to be his instruments (along with others who do his will without knowing that they do) in working for the removal of the causes of strife.

In a few weeks' time I go to India to lecture on 'The Overcoming of Evil'. I shall be hoping to find out more about Buddhist and Hindu resources for doing something about the world's ills. But I hope too to speak of Christian resources – the resources of God's forgiveness and transforming power – the spiritual resources of grace and love and peace which I hope we have all discovered to some degree and which I think we should hope will eventually prevail. For this is God's world and believers in the God of Easter should have the confidence that in the end all will be well.

32

WHAT ARE WE TO THINK ABOUT DON CUPITT?

It is not my usual practice in a sermon to hold forth about my friends and colleagues; but this term, having put myself down to preach twice, I think I am going to have to consider first the phenomenon of Don Cupitt and, second, that of Bishop David Jenkins. Both men have sought the maximum publicity for very controversial views and have certainly succeeded both in capturing attention and making us think. And to be made to think, at least, is a good thing.

1 *The Sea of Faith*
Now I must not assume that you have all seen the excellent television series, *The Sea of Faith* – I mean it is excellent television! – still less that you have read Don Cupitt's writings, the very explicit series of five articles in the *Listener* which he has written to accompany his series and explain his own position, and his recent books, including the one entitled *The Sea of Faith* (BBC), which goes with the television series. For the benefit of those who have not seen the programmes – and perhaps for the benefit of those who have, since I suspect that many believers as well as unbelievers will have found the programmes by themselves pretty confusing – I shall begin by giving a brief summary of what Don Cupitt is doing in these programmes and of his views about religion and Christianity.

Taking his cue and his title from Matthew Arnold's poem 'Dover Beach', in which the poet compares the modern erosion of religious belief to an ebbing tide, he attempts to give an account, largely through vivid sketches of key figures in the rise of modern science, philosophy, psychology and historical criticism, of the breakdown of not only the medieval, but the whole traditional world view, the classical

Christian conception of God, the universe and man. And then, through another series of portraits of key figures, he tries to show the religious mind reacting to and adjusting to the modern scientific world view – chiefly by interiorizing and subjectivizing religion, making it a matter of our own values, ideals and aspirations, including spiritual disciplines and ethical commitments in the interests of and in the light of those ideals.

It is clear, more from the writings than from the television series, that the Dean of Emmanuel has come to accept as a consequence of modern science and philosophy since Kant that it is no longer possible to believe in an objective God, another spiritual world and life after death. But the interest of his position lies in the fact that, far from thinking that this means that he has lost his faith, he thinks he has discovered what faith really means, what religion and Christianity are really all about and what talk of God, the spirit and eternity have always really meant. They are all, he says, expressive of and instruments of commitment to Christian values. And so he happily continues to use the language of religion, of prayer, or worship, and takes part in the services and rituals of the Church, all as a way of affirming and expressing his allegiance to and reinforcing a highly ethical and religious way of life. Indeed he remains, in a sense, a very religious man – much more so than I am.

He says, please note, that he believes in God; for this, he says, is what belief in God really means. Anything else, says he, is superstition.

He also thinks that this view is where all religion is going and is bound to go in the future. And I really think that he sees his role as a prophetic one, pointing to what Christianity must and can only become.

Well, as I say, it is good television, and I have greatly enjoyed seeing Don Cupitt prowling about Galileo's study and sailing up to Jung's castle on Lake Geneva, paddling in a dug-out canoe up to Albert Schweitzer's Lambarene, and

strolling through the Danish woods where Kierkegaard
walked and thought. Also, I am bound to say that he has
presented the significance of figures such as Galileo, Des-
cartes, Freud and Marx extremely well. As I say, it makes
you think and there is no doubting the problems raised by the
rise of modern science, philosophy and historiography for
faith.

2 Some main criticisms

But anyone who knows about these things is bound to feel a
certain irritation, indeed a string of irritations with this
project. In the first place it is irritating to have the medieval
world view or rather the whole of Christian thought prior to
1700 presented so monolithically and crudely as though it
were nothing but a Victorian child's picture book view of the
universe. The fact is that the Church fathers, St Anselm, St
Thomas Aquinas, Luther and Calvin, to name but a few,
were already grappling, with a high degree of sophistication
and in several radically different ways, with the problems of
relating our knowledge of God to our knowledge of the world
about us. But much more serious than that historical point is
the way in which the second group of key figures, chosen to
illustrate the religious response to the rise of modern science,
is selected it seems, purely in order to lead up to Don Cupitt's
own view as the only possible reaction to the problem which
modernity poses to religion. The fact is that Pascal, Jung,
Schweitzer, Kierkegaard, to say nothing of Annie Besant
(and Wittgenstein, whose views will dazzle us, apparently,
next Wednesday) are all highly ambiguous figures, whose
religious views are capable of being understood much more
objectively in terms of a response to an objective God than
Mr Cupitt will allow.

Not only is this second list of key figures highly selective
and not only are they interpreted in only one of the possible
ways in which they can be understood, most irritating of all is
the Dean of Emmanuel's complete failure to give any

161

indication that there are other ways of tackling this great debate between science and religion, and between philosophy and religion, and other equally important figures who could have been chosen to illustrate the resolution of the science/religion debate. I think of the splendid book by Arthur Peacocke, the Dean of Clare, *Creation and the World of Science* (Oxford), as an example of the very different moves that can be made in this game.

But the main objection to Don Cupitt's views is that, in my opinion, they are nearly all false. I think that, for all the marvels of modern science in discovering and explaining the basic constituents of matter, the history of cosmic evolution, and the causal interconnections of events and processes in the world, there remain very good reasons for believing in an infinite objective God, the creator of all there is and the source of all value in the universe, including the value of our life as persons. I think the history of religions, including Christ and the Bible, and our own religious experience are far more plausibly explained in terms of a spiritual power or resource, not our own, that saves us from evil and destruction, transforms us and fashions us for eternity – all of these things being things we cannot do for ourselves.

3 *Limits to tolerance*
Obviously all this could be spelled out and defended at length. But even if I were to keep you here till midnight doing just that, there would still be more to be said and I cannot fight shy of mentioning the much more delicate, indeed embarrassing, fact that this is not just a dispute between two Cambridge lecturers in the philosophy of religion over the essence of religion and over whether there exists an objective God. For both Don Cupitt and I are priests of the Church of England and Deans of our respective college chapels, and here we are giving radically different accounts of what Christianity is.

Now of course there must be room for a variety of

interpretations of central Christian beliefs and for much criticism and debate within the Church and especially within theology. I myself would want to criticize many aspects of traditional Church teaching and many ways in which Christianity is preached and taught today. But there are limits; for I am not just saying what I think as opposed to what Don Cupitt thinks. As priests of the Church we are both authorized to preach and teach a faith which is not our private property, but the faith of a particular community – a changing, developing community of faith, maybe, but not a completely amorphous hotch-potch of individuals' bright ideas. And all I can say is that if I came to believe that religion is not concerned with an objective God, nor with the resources of grace from beyond this finite world, nor with a God-centred life that extends beyond death, I should feel bound to resign my orders, and leave the Church.

As I say, I find it rather embarrassing to have to say such things. But if a friend and colleague and fellow priest says publicly and loudly that what I preach and what the Church for the most part preaches is superstition, then I have to react, not just on my own behalf but on your behalf and on the Church's behalf. And I think it very important that the Church's leaders and official bodies should publicly and explicitly dissociate themselves from the Dean of Emmanuel's views. I do not say that there should be a heresy trial or that Don Cupitt should be deprived of his orders. The Church's experience of such things is much too negative and horrible and unchristian for that to be contemplated seriously, I think. We can surely tolerate this anomalous gadfly in our midst. After all, as I have said more than once, he certainly makes us think and it is splendid television. But it is not the Church's teaching and I really do not think that it is true.

33

WHAT ARE WE TO THINK ABOUT DAVID JENKINS?

Unlike my animadversions at the beginning of term on the Dean of Emmanuel, my treatment of the Bishop of Durham this evening will be more positive than negative. For, despite a certain tendency towards infelicity of expression and, more seriously, a certain insensitivity to the effect of unguarded remarks by a public figure, Bishop David Jenkins has said many true and important things both about Christian doctrine and about Christian social ethics. I propose to comment briefly on the doctrinal matters, then to say something about the issues of social ethical concern.

The Bishop's admittedly rather crude remarks about the virgin birth and the resurrection were made with two very positive aims in mind. The first was to encourage Christians to focus their attention on the heart of the doctrines of the incarnation and the resurrection rather than on their periphery, and the second was to teach Christians to realize that, provided the heart of the doctrines is understood and believed, we must be tolerant of diversity in interpretation of the periphery. (You will recall that it was because the Dean of Emmanuel's views involve a total denial of the traditional *heart* of the Christian doctrine of God that I rejected them so uncompromisingly in my previous address.) Now there is no doubt in my mind that David Jenkins, like all the bishops in the Church of England, whatever certain ignorant and foolish peers may say, firmly believes in God. Moreover he is one of the ablest exponents of the doctrine of the Trinity, and when he says, as he said the other day, admittedly in somewhat unespicopal plain language, 'Anyone who says that I do not believe in the resurrection and in the incarnation is a liar', I believe him.

1 *The Virgin Birth*

What then was the fuss about? Let me try to explain the matter in my own words. Belief in the incarnation is belief that the man Jesus was not just a great prophet and teacher, but our God himself, in the person of his Word or Son, coming into our midst and living out a human life and dying a human death, in order to make himself known to us, and in order to win our repentance, our love and our commitment in return. Humanity – not humanity in general but a particular human life – by the incarnation is taken into God, and we, as Christ's followers and fellow-heirs, we too are drawn into the life of God for ever. The incarnation was both a historical and a trans-historical event. It happened at a particular time and place. But at the same time God's coming into history and his taking humanity into God cannot possibly be spoken of as just a historical event. It was an eternal, supernatural, event as well.

Now traditionally the incarnation was thought to have been marked by the virginal conception of our Lord in the womb of Mary his mother. All the Bishop of Durham wanted to say about that was that, in the post-critical age of biblical interpretation, we cannot possibly insist on every Christian taking that traditional story literally – (a) because it is somewhat insecurely based in the possible legendary birth narratives of Matthew and Luke (and nowhere else in the New Testament), and (b) because we cannot, in serious theology, suppose that God could only become incarnate by abrogating the normal operations of nature, as though nature were somehow foreign territory to its creator and had to be invaded from without. The Bishop was trying to teach Christians that such critical reflections are permissible within the Church, and I entirely agree with him that it would be lunacy to try to ban them. In fact I myself, who am a resolute defender of the doctrine of the incarnation, am disposed to think the virgin birth story may be a legendary expression of the truth that Jesus of Nazareth was the Son of God incarnate.

2 *The Resurrection*

Belief in the resurrection is belief that Jesus Christ, after his death on the cross, was raised to life again by God the Father, was manifested to the disciples in his risen body, and now lives for ever in heaven, at the same time coming to us in the power of his Spirit to bind us to him in the fellowship of the sons and daughters of God. The resurrection too was both a historical and a trans-historical event. It happened at a particular time and place, but burst the bounds of nature and history, indeed anticipating the end of nature and history. In this respect it is very different and much more central than the virgin birth.

Now on any serious view of the resurrection, the risen body of Jesus was transformed – as ours will be, in the language of St Paul – from a physical body to a spiritual body, no longer locatable in our space nor interacting physically with physical objects in our space. Traditionally, of course, that trans-historical event of the resurrection, in addition to having taken place at a particular time and place in history, was held to have left historical traces – an empty tomb (and perhaps a shroud) – and to have been followed by visible appearances to the disciples and others on several occasions. These appearances are hardly in doubt, though many of us will interpret them as objective, God-given, visions of Christ in his risen, spiritual body. Moreover the spiritual nature of the Lord's risen body may dispose us to be more sympathetic to stories of its passing through closed doors than to probably legendary embellishments concerning the eating of fish by the lakeside.

But again the Bishop of Durham's point in questioning the necessity of imposing even belief in the empty tomb on all Christians is the manifest fact that the resurrection was not a mere physical resuscitation and that at some point we have to postulate a supernatural transformation of the physical body into the spiritual body of the risen Christ; for, as Paul again so wisely said, 'Flesh and blood cannot inherit the kingdom of God'. Actually I think the evidence for the tomb having been found empty (unlike the evidence for the virgin birth) is pretty strong. I dare say I am more disposed to affirm it than Bishop Jenkins is. But again, critical freedom of interpretation must be permitted at this point. If you ask me what happened to the physical body, I am bound to say, I do not know. Maybe its physical substance was annihiliated as the resurrection body was assumed or rather given. But I do not know. All I know is that the resurrection is more than – well *I* would not say fiddling about with bones – I do blush for the Bishop at that – but the resurrection is certainly not to be thought of as a merely physical resuscitation.

You will appreciate that the Bishop's insistence on freedom of interpretation where the details of the biblical narratives are concerned, albeit within an agreed framework of doctrinal belief, does imply acceptance of biblical criticism and a refusal to bind the Church to a literal view of everything that is in the Bible. Well, if Christians think that the Church or the clergy or the bishops can or should be bound to a literal view of everything that is in the Bible, they are playing on a losing wicket and need to be taught otherwise by the Bishops, I hope, as well as by the theologians.

3 *The miners' strike*
Let me turn to the miners' strike. Bishop Jenkins embarked upon his episcopate with a rousing enthronement sermon on hope and reconciliation and on the need for a responsible readiness for compromise in matters of social and political concern such as the current miners' strike. He did not shrink from applying his message to that issue – how could a new Bishop of *Durham* avoid it? – blaming both sides and the Government for both incompetence and intransigence, and pleading for a greater concern for the social consequences of economic policies. He ended with a reference to the incarnation and the principle it exemplifies of getting involved in

what is going on, and transforming it from within. The sermon was greeted in Durham Cathedral by prolonged applause – a thing that has never happened to one of my sermons!

The Press, of course, seemed only interested in one perhaps unfortunate phrase, for which again I blush – slightly – and which I propose to ignore. What matters is the question whether the Bishop – and later the Archbishop of Canterbury – were right to get involved in current political disputes to the extent of ticking off the Government.

The Dean of Peterhouse (another remarkable denizen of the menagerie of Cambridge Deans) is of the opinion that the Church's task is to turn men and women to God and that bishops should preach about spiritual things, not the policies of the day. But Bishop Jenkins did preach about God and spiritual things. Moreover spiritual things include, supremely, love, and we are taught that you cannot love God without loving your neighbour. And loving your neighbour cannot just be a matter of benevolence and charity to individuals. We and our neighbours in this country are members of a society which, while not as bad as some societies in the world today, is very far from being all sweetness and light; and the Church must bear witness to God's law of love when governments and politicians as well as business men and individuals flout it. (We are also members of a world community, whose divisions between rich and poor are so flagrantly obvious in these days of the Ethiopian famine that really we should be talking about that and asking what loving our neighbour on a world scale means rather than about relatively trivial matters like the British miners' strike.)

Still we are supposed to love our neighbours in our own society and it seems to me not only that it is quite proper but that it is their positive duty, for bishops and other Church leaders to speak out against the attitudes and policies that foment division, create or ignore need, and inhibit love. The plain fact is that economic and social policies can have these effects – fomenting division, creating or ignoring need and inhibiting love. What I call the sphere of Christian social ethical concern is inextricably bound up with the gospel of reconciliation and love, and so with spirituality. On the Christian view you cannot have either spirituality or mysticism without love; and it is reflection on what love means that inevitably leads the Church, its leaders and its members – all of them – to care about things like justice and human rights.

It is often held that the Church should stick to questions of principal and general attitude and leave the details of economics and politics to the professionals. There is something to be said for this view, at least where the different policies and the different parties are not obviously evil through and through. Economics and politics are complicated things and it is usually a mistake for the Church to commit itself absolutely to one side of a political dispute unless the rights and wrongs of an issue are absolutely clear and beyond question. But we should not forget the terrible examples of Church spokesmen for the Nazis in the 30s or for Apartheid in South Africa today. Mercifully we are not in that kind of situation in these islands and the miners' strike is far from being a black or white affair. But there are worrying signs – the increasing polarization of left and right, a readiness to pursue economic goals irrespective of social consequences, a readiness on the part of those in work to ignore the plight of those who, through no fault of their own, cannot get work, and the increasing gap between a prosperous south of England and an impoverished north.

But in any case the Bishop of Durham's sermon was not a one-sided denunciation. It was a plea for compromise, reconciliation and concern for the life of communities blighted by rapid economic and technological change. If bishops cannot call attention to such things and press the Government to care more about such things and actively show more compassion, I cannot for the life of me think what they are supposed to talk about. For the religion of the incarnation insists that God himself gets involved in such things and the religion of the resurrection insists that we should never give up hope for a better world. Our ultimate hope may be for heaven, but that hope is of such a character, revealed as it is in the story of Jesus Christ, as always to reflect back upon and inspire our hope and our action in this world.

4 *Verdict*

So really I do think that David Jenkins is, on balance, a good thing. Both in doctrine and in social ethical concern he is exercising a commendable teaching and pastoral ministry, and I find it refreshing to have some bishops in the Church of England who are not afraid to call a spade a spade, even though I might be happier if they refrained from calling it, in church at least, a bloody shovel.

One final point: I have said nothing about the curious coincidence that a few days after the consecration of Bishop Jenkins, the south transept of York Minster was struck by lightning. The silly superstitious nonsense that found its way even into the correspondence columns of *The Times* was, as the Archbishop of York pointed out, strong evidence of the need for the sort of teaching that the new Bishop of Durham was giving. We need to teach Christians to get out of their heads entirely the superstitious idea that the God and Father of our Lord Jesus Christ is the sort of God who sends thunderbolts in the direction of mildly controversial bishops, or that, in any case, that kind of conception of how God acts in the world has any place in a mature Christian faith.

34

COMMEMORATION OF BENEFACTORS

We meet here this evening for the Commemoration of Benefactors as members of an institution which many people would regard as a very prestigious one. This university and this college are very ancient and very powerful institutions. And I think that many would say that we have every reason to be proud of being members of this place. Its buildings, its traditions, its achievements, its libraries, its community of scholars constitute something indeed to give thanks for. To be part of this institution can be a source of great pleasure and, in a sense, security to its members, though like all big institutions, it can be demanding and exacting, and somewhat overpowering. Nevertheless, it is against the background of its many positive qualities that members of the college turn their attention this evening to the five centuries of history that lie behind it, and give thanks for what has been given and achieved by so many excellent people over so many years, people whose inheritance we now enjoy.

1 *The University and the Church*
I draw this picture of a strong and honoured institution in order to contrast it with the Church. The Church could claim a much longer and a much more impressive list of benefactors than those to be named in a few moments time. But to read such a list might be thought to have a hollow ring today; for no one can deny that the contemporary Church is weak. We Christians may be inheritors of what the saints and doctors of the Church have left behind them, but far from enjoying membership of a strong and secure institution in the forefront of society, we find ourselves thought of as irrelevant and uninfluential, driven to wondering whether the

Church will survive into the twenty-first century.

The temptation to appeal to common standards of human excellence in the Church's benefactors certainly exists. For example, it is sometimes suggested that the chapel ought to be turned into squash courts or that the theology faculty ought to be abolished in favour of more useful subjects. I know I should be tempted to reply by saying that you cannot so lightly dismiss an institution which throughout its long history has fostered men like Augustine, Aquinas, Luther and Karl Barth. I know from my own experience that I enjoyed just as liberal an education, just as profound a commerce with great minds, just as serious a preoccupation with great issues in my theological education here in Cambridge as I did in my philosophical education at Oxford. I could also call as witnesses many great musicians, many great writers, many great artists, past and present, whose inspiration and influence have been primarily Christian. The list of benefactors would be long. It would include plenty of names from the twentieth century, just as the list of the College's benefactors does. I cannot believe that it is a waste of time to master the thought of Barth and Tillich and Teilhard de Chardin, to name but a few. The poetry of T.S. Eliot and the novels of Graham Greene and William Golding do not, it seems to me, reflect a myopic or narrow view of life. And so the argument could continue.

I say it would be a temptation to argue in this way. For not only do these considerations do absolutely nothing to alter the plain fact of the Church's weakness in our contemporary world; they also involve the use of false criteria, wrong standards by which to judge the significance of the Church today or at any time.

2 The genius and the apostle

At this point I should like to mention a short essay by Soren Kierkegaard entitled 'Of the Difference between a Genius and an Apostle'. In it he complains that Christians of his time

172

have sold the pass. They use quite the wrong standards in speaking, say, of St Paul. 'They talk in exalted terms of St Paul's brilliance and profundity, of his beautiful similes and so on. . . ', whereas in fact these qualities are quite beside the point; for St Paul is an apostle, and to praise him as a genius is to do him a great disservice, because it conceals his distinctive work. Genius is a human category, and Kierkegaard certainly does not want to disparage it; but an apostle is what he is solely in virtue of his divine calling. He may be the very reverse of a genius, an extremely weak and feeble person, possessed of no great human qualities at all, and yet be used by God as a witness to his revelation and action and purpose in the world. Kierkegaard, in fact, goes further and says that to put the apostle and the genius on a level is all part and parcel with the tendency to put God on a level with man – in his own words, God is put '. . . on the same level as geniuses, poets and thinkers whose sayings are judged from a purely aesthetic or philosophic point of view; and then, if the thing is well said, the man is a genius – and if it is unusually well said, then God said it.'

I do not wish to tie us down too closely to Kierkegaard. There are difficulties in his understanding of what faith means. Let us simply take from him this one idea: that to compare the apostle with the genius is to use the wrong criteria, and miss the distinctive calling of the apostle, which is to point away from himself to the reality of God and to the claims of God.

3 Confusion of standards

I imagine that you see the application of this point to what I was saying about the difference between the university and the Church. For precisely the same confusion of standards is involved if we attempt to defend the Church or its theology by talking about the culture it has fostered, or the philosophical profundity of its great thinkers. One could even go on to say that the relative weakness and feebleness of the Church

173

have the positive role of forcing us back to ask ourselves what is the real function of the Church, now that its position in our culture and society are seen, humanly speaking, to be impermanent and unessential. The answer will be precisely the same as it was in the case of Kierkegaard's apostle. The Church exists solely in so far as it points away from itself to the reality of God and to the claims of God.

I cannot resist adding that the same thing applies to what is said about Jesus. There is a tendency for some biblical scholars to claim that they can discern, behind the distinctive concepts of New Testament thought, the 'great creative mind' of Jesus. I cannot see that it is our business to go around praising Jesus as a 'great creative mind'. Surely this is why Karl Barth suggests that actually Jesus may not have been a particularly interesting person, humanly speaking. Only in so far as Jesus was utterly transparent to God can we take an interest in him now. He was most truly the revelation of God, when humanly speaking he was nothing – despised and deserted, nailed to the cross.

So we must, I think, let ourselves be faced with the question whether we are prepared to listen to the apostle, or whether we are quite happy sitting at the genius' feet. I repeat that no disparagement of geniuses is intended and certainly no disparagement of our benefactors for whom we have every reason to praise God and be thankful tonight. But the question remains. The very existence of the apostle sets a question mark against our satisfaction and our security. There is an inescapable dilemma. I remember this coming home to me most poignantly as a result of an anecdote of my teacher, Professor Donald MacKinnon. He had been invited to the funeral of the head of one of the Oxford colleges, a man whose atheistic views were widely known. He had found himself incapable of attending the religious ceremony on account of its hypocrisy, and as he walked about outside, he asked himself whether he would rather have been that man with all his academic excellence and professional eminence, a

174

man with many books to his credit and a successful career behind – or an unknown, humble, ordinary man, dying with the name of Christ on his lips.

Of course, this is not an alternative between which one has to choose, but maybe it makes us ask ourselves where we stand.

The Church must judge itself by different standards from those applicable to the college and the university. If it attempts to overcome its present weakness in our society and culture by means of geniuses and benefactors it will become weak in a much more radical and disastrous sense; it will lose its apostolic status. Its transparency to God will become frosted over, and it will desert as it has done often enough in the past the way of the cross. The paradox created by this conflict of criteria has never been better exploited than by St Paul when he insists that God's strength is made known through weakness, and at the same time affirms that the foolishness of God is wiser than men. That these affirmations must continue to be made is the only ultimate justification for the existence of the theology faculty in this university and of this chapel in the college.

35

BRIDESHEAD REVISITED

I do not think it inappropriate to reflect for a few moments on Evelyn Waugh's novel, *Brideshead Revisited*, so marvellously filmed and acted in the television dramatization. For the novel's theme was described by Waugh as 'the operation of divine grace on a group of diverse but closely connected characters'. And what better subject for our reflections here in Queens' chapel at the end of another academic year than the operation of divine grace on a group of diverse but closely connected characters?

I shall indeed be concentrating on the religious theme – on the oddities as well as the profundities of Waugh's treatment of the theme. But of course the novel deals with other topics too. 'My theme is memory. . .' the book's narrator says – and that too is a theme not out of place in this Eucharist – this act done 'as a remembrance' of Christ's death and resurrection – to say nothing of other memories that may come crowding into some of your minds as you prepare to leave this place. The novel is also about friendship and love – and about human tragedy, about the troubles people bring upon themselves – 'and those', said Waugh in a letter at the time of writing, 'are mainly the demons of sex and drink. . .' Well, I shall say a little about all these things too, though not very much. One thing I will not say anything about is the theme of class, which some people find unattractive in *Brideshead Revisited*. 'I am writing a very beautiful book, to bring tears, about very rich, beautiful, high born people who live in palaces. . .' wrote Waugh in the same letter. Well, that style of life is past and gone. I think it silly to get het up about it. We can treat it aesthetically now and contemplate it with detached amused tolerance and not with resentment. It really does not belong to our world and can safely be ignored, at least as a theme for serious reflection.

1 *Memory*

Let me begin with the theme of memory. As I say we are engaged in a liturgy of remembrance in this Eucharist. We re-present the saving acts that have made us what we are as Christians. And in this Eucharist – this thanksgiving – we bring to God all our memories, for forgiveness and for blessing, for healing, as well, as well as in gratitude. I hope that those of you leaving Queens' will have more to be thankful for than to be sorry for when you look back over your years in this place, but either way you will need, even if you do not want, to integrate this bit of the past into your lives. And I suspect that even those who have had their troubles here will not have been unaffected by the medieval and Tudor buildings, by the shafts of sunlight across Cloister Court, by the river and the trees, by the books and all the memorials treasured here of many generations of men, as we say in the Commemoration of Benefactors.

And of course you will thank God for the friendships you have made and enjoyed during these years. Human beings need good memories, healed memories, they need good roots, and of course they need friends. I do not think I am just advocating nostalgia about Cambridge like that of Waugh for Oxford. I do not suppose many of you will want to say of your time at Queens', '*et in Arcadia ego*', as Charles Ryder did of his all too brief sojourn in Oxford; and anyway his 'Arcady' soon turned sour, and his memories called for much healing; but there are good things here, as there (Oxford, I mean), on which the mind and the memory can draw, and we should be thankful – in this Eucharist – that we have enjoyed them for so long. Christians ought not to be coy about enjoying what is good. For everything that is good is of God.

Maybe you think I am muddling up memories sacred and profane in speaking in the same breath of this eucharistic memorial and our memories of university life. The subtitle of *Brideshead Revisited* is 'The Sacred and Profane Memories of Captain Charles Ryder'. And clearly some of his memories were only too sacred and some were only too profane. But here we come across one of the main problems those beautiful people in *Brideshead Revisited* got snarled up over: for them, in a way, the sacred was too sacred and the profane too profane and the gulf between the sacred and the profane too absolute and vast. Maybe it was just because they could not integrate the earthly into the heavenly that things went so wrong for them, and their earthly loves became so profane in the bad, anti-religious sense.

177

2 *The sacred and the profane*

I am being quite serious when I plead for integration of the sacred and the profane, the heavenly and the earthly. I suggest that if we can find God in and not apart from our earthly loves – love of place and love of people – then the latter will not cut loose and become demonic as they did for Sebastian and Julia (and Charles in his rather feeble way). In saying all this I am drawing on an address by the former Master of Gonville and Caius College, Joseph Needham, which has greatly influenced my thinking on these matters, an address called 'Love Sacred and Profane', where he argues against the traditional opposition of the different forms of love. And that is really what I want to say about friendship and love. 'To know and love one other human being is the root of all wisdom', says Charles Ryder in *Brideshead Revisited*. But that all turned sour, became profane in the pejorative sense, turned in upon itself and, at least in the short run, led to misery and ruin, both in the case of Sebastian and in that of Julia. The love of Charles and Julia, the 'orphans of the storm', was an adulterous love, a forbidden love, and it could not survive the pressures of conscience or of grace. I fear that that is what can happen to our earthly loves. It does not always or necessarily happen, of course, but it can happen when they are seen as rivals to the divine love instead of pointers to the divine love, indeed expressions, media and instruments of the divine love, which is how things should be.

Now much the same sort of thing must be said about those demons of drink and sex to which Waugh refers. The fact is they *are* not demons but can easily become so. I sometimes think we drink too much at Cambridge. Not that I am seriously disposed to take the pledge – though there are times when the baying of hearties across the courts and the sheer grossness of young people incapacitated by drink turn my thoughts in that direction. Occasionally, when called out on pernoctation duty, I shake my head in sadness at the temporary departure of the image of God from the face of a human being thus incapacitated. But, as the poet, John Selden, said, 'Tis not the drinking that is to be blamed, but the excess'; and I hope that we can learn to appreciate as one of God's gifts, not to be abused, 'the wine that maketh glad the heart of man' (Psalm 104.15). Mercifully I have only rarely come upon cases of chronic alcoholism. Such cases call for sensitive and compassionate treatment and recourse to professional help, not keeping the victim a prisoner and depriving him of money, which was Lady Marchmain's policy where Sebastian was concerned, nor quietly slipping him some money or a bottle and doing nothing at all to help, which was Charles Ryder's feeble policy for his friend.

As for 'the demon of sex' as Waugh calls it, I will only repeat that sex *is* not demonic, though it can become so. But where it is the expression of deep commitment and faithful life-giving love, it is indeed of God and a place where the divine is to be found. In such a case we may endorse Charles Ryder's saying that 'to know and love one other human being is the root of all wisdom'. The deep sadness of *Brideshead Revisited* lies in the failure of all the characters to find and realize that truth, and in the chasm that opened up for them, partly throught their own fault, between the sacred and the profane.

3 *Grace*

But now it is time to speak of grace. For *Brideshead Revisited* is a religious novel and is first and foremost about the operation of divine grace. Now with all due respect to our Roman Catholic friends among us, I very much doubt that even they will be particularly happy about the religion of Lord Brideshead and Lady Marchmain. Waugh himself makes the point very well: 'D'you know, Bridey, if I ever felt for a moment like becoming a Catholic, I should only have to talk to you for five minutes to be cured. . .' 'It's odd that you should say that. I've heard it before from other people. It's

179

one of the many reasons why I don't think I should make a good priest. It's something in the way my mind works, I suppose.' And as for Lady Marchmain, we are all, I imagine, appalled by the air of martyrdom with which she exerts her moral blackmail on her children and their friends. But even Cordelia was aware of that: 'I sometimes think when people wanted to hate God they hated mummy.''What do you mean by that, Cordelia?' 'Well you see, she was saintly, but she wasn't a saint. No one could really hate a saint, could they? They can't really hate God either. When they want to hate him and his saints they have to find something like themselves and pretend it's God and hate that.'

But the main religious idea of the novel is the one Waugh clearly had in mind when he spoke of the novel as being about 'the operation of divine grace'. It is summed up by the title of the third and final part of the book, 'A twitch upon the thread'. This is in fact a quotation from one of G.K. Chesterton's Father Brown stories – a story which Lady Marchmain is reading aloud on the terrible evening when Sebastian's alcoholism first becomes apparent. Father Brown says of the thief in the story, 'I caught him with an unseen hook and an invisible line which is long enough to let him wander to the ends of the world and still to bring him back with a twitch of the thread.' This then became a metaphor for the way God never lets his wayward creatures fall right out of his hand. One way or another they are all brought back, Julia to her conscience and her faith, Sebastian to his quasi-monastic existence in Morocco (Cordelia's description of this in her last conversation with Charles was described by Waugh in a letter as the theoloical clue to the meaning of the novel), and Lord Marchmain, most surprisingly of all, to a reconciliation with the Church by making the sign of the cross just before he dies, and even Charles Ryder to a new-found faith and acceptance of what has happened, when, years later, he says a prayer in the chapel at Brideshead, where his brigade has found itself encamped.

What are we to make of this idea of 'a twitch upon the thread'? I must say I do not like it very much as a metaphor for the operation of grace. It is too impersonal a metaphor. I think the more we learn of God's ways as they are revealed in Christ the more we are bound to think of them as the ways of an utterly gracious personal relation, a love endowed with infinite patience and concern. The prodigal son was not restored to his father by a twitch upon the thread but by an inner movement of the heart, a recognition of the shambles he had made of his life, and an awareness that he had a home to which he could return. But, of course the story of the victory of grace in the motley characters in *Brideshead* is a better and more personal story than the metaphor of a twitch upon the thread might suggest. And the idea that God does let us be to make or mar our lives and yet does not ever let us go is a deeply Christian idea, and one on which we here might well reflect as we ponder about our own lives and those of our friends.

Of course we do encounter some people who betray no sign at all of the operation of grace. Of the main characters in *Brideshead* only Rex Mottram comes into this category, and a pretty objectionable specimen of thoroughly secular man he is. (I can think of much nicer examples here at Queens' among both Fellows and undergraduates.) But most of us here in this chapel tonight will, I guess, at some time in our lives, have experienced some inkling of the operation of divine grace, some sense of wonder at the mystery of the world's and of our own existence, some sense of objective value and of the spiritual dimension to life, some revelation of the meaning and the possibilities of life as we consider the example of Christ and his saints, some sense of the call to be channels of divine grace to one another. And no matter how far we or our friends find ourselves drifting from the faith of the Church – for good or for bad reasons – the fact remains that 'underneath are the everlasting arms' and neither we nor our friends can be lost for ever.

I think we need this faith that in the end grace cannot fail – that the source of all being and value will not let us go, but will, one way or another, restore us again – not by a twitch of the thread, as though we were puppets on a string, nor by pious manipulation à la Lady Marchmain – but by a patient untiring love, the love that loved us into life, the love that gave himself for us, the love for which we were made. You remember Francis Thompson's poem, *The Hound of Heaven*:

> I fled Him, down the nights and down the days;
> I fled Him, down the arches of the years;
> I fled Him, down the labyrinthine ways
> Of my own mind; and in the mist of tears
> I hid from Him, and under running laughter.

But the poet is pursued, 'with unhurrying chase, and unperturbed pace, deliberate speed, majestic instancy. . .' and finally

> 'Halts by me that footfall.
> Is my gloom, after all
> Shade of His hand, outstretched caressingly?
> 'Ah, fondest, blindest, weakest,
> I am He whom thou seekest!
> Thou dravest love from thee, who dravest Me.'

I think that captures rather better than 'a twitch upon the thread' the notion that pervades *Brideshead* of a grace that is sure to prevail in the end. I hope that you will find that love at the heart of things. I hope you will not have to go through the kind of troubles that Sebastian, Charles and Julia brought upon themselves before you find or are found by grace. But even if you do get so ensnarled, I trust that, in the end, like Charles in the chapel of Brideshead you will rediscover the 'small red flame' – the flame of faith – 'burning anew among the old stones'.

Other Mowbray Sermon Outlines
Series Editor: D. W. Cleverley Ford

Preaching through the Acts of the Apostles: D. W. Cleverley
Ford
Preaching through the Life of Christ: D. W. Cleverley Ford
Preaching through the Prophets: John B. Taylor
Preaching through the Psalms: D. W. Cleverley Ford
Preaching through Saint Paul: Derrick Greeves
More Preaching from the New Testament: D. W. Cleverley
Ford
More Preaching from the Old Testament: D. W. Cleverley
Ford
Preaching on Special Occasions Volume 1: D. W. Cleverley
Ford
Preaching on Special Occasions Volume 2: D. W. Cleverley
Ford
Preaching on Special Occasions Volume 3: Edward H.
Patey
Preaching through the Christian Year
Vol. 7 by Alan Dunstan
Vol. 8 by Frank Colquhoun
Vol. 9 by Robert Martineau
Preaching at the Parish Communion
ASB Gospels – Sundays: Year One: Dennis Runcorn
ASB Gospels – Sundays: Year Two: Raymond Wilkinson
ASB Epistles – Sundays: Year One: Robin Osborne
ASB Epistles – Sundays: Year Two: Dennis Runcorn